W9-BVI-001

HOW TO PREACH TO PEOPLE'S NEEDS

HOW TO PREACH TO PEOPLE'S NEEDS

EDGAR N. JACKSON

NEW YORK   ABINGDON PRESS   NASHVILLE

B

SET UP, PRINTED, AND BOUND BY THE
PARTHENON PRESS, AT NASHVILLE,
TENNESSEE. UNITED STATES OF AMERICA

TO

THE REV. EDGAR S. JACKSON

This book is dedicated to my father
who from my earliest memory to this day
has made preaching an important healing instrument.

PREFACE

In the pages that follow I have attempted to take areas of human need and deal with them in the light of the insight that recent years have been able to furnish. The approach from the pulpit is suggested and sermon résumés are used for illustrations. I feel that this helps to make clear what is implied in preaching to human needs.

I wish to express a debt of gratitude for the helpful criticism and guidance of such teachers of preaching as Hugh Black, Lynn Harold Hough, Harry Emerson Fosdick, John Schroeder and Halford E. Luccock. Also to those persons who have reacted to my preaching in one way or another for more than two decades, I express appreciation. Parts of the Introduction and Chapter III are based on articles I wrote for *Pastoral Psychology* and *The Pastor*. I am grateful to the publishers of these periodicals for permission to adapt this material.

With respect for the traditions of the pulpit and a concern that the valuable tool of pulpit utterance be kept sharpened by the best insights into the nature and needs of humanity, this book is presented, with the prayer that it may help to bring pulpit and pew closer together in a healing, redeeming, and soul-saving relationship.

EDGAR N. JACKSON

CONTENTS

21559

9

HOW TO PREACH TO PEOPLE'S NEEDS

Preaching the Healing Word

Preaching is an ancient and respected art. Its long history evidences a continuity of concern with man's needs. This concern has often been combined with an awareness of contemporary resources for meeting such needs. As new tools of understanding have been developed, they have been adapted to the use of the pulpit.

Our day has developed a great amount of understanding of the personality structure and human behavior that condition our approach to persons. This has been clearly shown by the effect of psychological insight into the practice of pastoral care and counseling.

However, there seems to have been no comparable effort to evaluate this new understanding as it relates to the pulpit and its effort to deal with human needs. Many pastors have used such knowledge in their own preaching, but there has been little or no interest in a study of these matters as they relate to the function of preaching as a therapeutic tool.

The use of the sermon as an instrument of group therapy is probably one of the oldest forms of ministry to the soul needs of mankind. The tribal rites and dances of the dim past undoubtedly served some comparable purpose in the lives of primitive people, but their primary concern was to give a consciousness of the group to the individual. Early preaching advanced a step toward making the members of the group conscious of their significance as individuals.

The Old Testament prophets made individual behavior a matter of concern in their messages. The problems of the group were individualized. Social sins were dramatized as the excesses of individuals. Righteousness was interpreted as the behavior of individuals who feared God and dealt justly with man.

The finest examples of preaching as a soul-healing force come from the ministry of Jesus. Here was life-situation preaching at its best. Commonplace situations were filled with meaning. People saw their own behavior dramatized. They felt their burdens lifted. They knew a closeness to God that gave their lives new value. They gained courage to face their weakness. They saw their failures not as a final catastrophe but as a steppingstone to new understanding. They sensed that the soul of man gained peace when it was at ease before God and other men. They found a key with which to resolve their hatred and pride in a genuine love and concern for others. In a word, they grew, under the preaching of Jesus, to a mature insight into their own natures and their relationship to their Creator.

From the example of Jesus there can be drawn certain requisite presuppositions for preaching as a form of group soul-healing. There was always the recognition of problems, and the possibility of solution. There was always understanding of the cause-effect relationship in living, so that the emphasis was on helping the individual to face the future, rather than condemning past behavior. Yet there was a consciousness of the power of a sense of guilt over both body and mind, and the need for soul purging through forgiveness. Further, there was a strong sense of the need for healing action that could fix new habit patterns in the life of the healed individual. And at the core of his preaching there was

12

a sense of concern, even compassion, that made the individual in the group feel that here was a friend to be trusted and followed.

Some modern experts on psychotherapy approach the idea of group practice as new and untried. Maurice Levine writes that "group psychotherapy is still in the experimental stage." To be sure, such techniques as spontaneous dramatic presentations of life problems may be new, but hardly the same could be said of group recreation, lectures, specially adapted visual techniques, and public worship. Karl A. Menninger admits that group psychotherapy "is of course implicit in the professional work of the minister. . . . It would be unscientific to ignore the fact that people do influence one another in groups and do respond to group situations." But the important preventive and healing potential of the thousands of worship services and the soul-healing effects of thousands of sermons each year are largely overlooked.

This ignoring of the healing effect of modern preaching may be significant. It may indicate that specialists in the field of ministering to sick souls judge the average minister to be inept, unconscious of the soul needs of his people, or incapable of meeting them satisfactorily through the medium of the sermon. While such a judgment may not be considered as entirely reasonable, it should lead those who preach to do some soul searching themselves. Suffice it to say that in order to be a qualified psychoanalyst it is important to be psychoanalyzed. The preacher who would give a message to heal souls must speak from a soul that knows the meaning and power of God's healing love.

Preaching to human needs demands the ability to visualize the congregation, even while the sermon is being prepared. Harold Roupp once compiled some telling figures concerning the congregation's idea of its needs. In response to specific questions nearly four thousand replies indicated that about half of the persons felt the major problems of their lives to be such personal matters as futility, insecurity, loneliness, marriage problems, sex, alcoholism, false ideas of religion and morals, inferiority, suffering, illness, frustrations, and guilt feelings. Nearly a quarter of the persons were concerned about family problems, child training, infidelity, separation, divorce, poor adjustment to marriage, religious differences in the home, and other problems that are symptoms of personal problems as they touch the lives of others. The remaining fraction were concerned with social, community, and national problems, or the more traditional religious concerns. It is significant that a major portion of the replies indicated personality problems that were symptoms of immaturity, inner conflicts, or aggressive behavior. The preacher who sees his people in terms of such needs has taken the first steps toward preaching with soul-healing power.

On the basis of compilations of averages it may be possible to get some concept of a cross section of your congregation. In a congregation of five hundred people, it is reasonable to assume that at least one hundred have been so recently bereaved as to feel an acute sense of loss. Probably a third of the married persons are facing problems of personality adjustment that may weaken or destroy their home life. At least half of the five hundred can be assumed to have problems of emotional adjustment to school, work, home, or community that endanger their happiness. Others may have neuroses ranging from alcohol addiction to lesser forms of obsessions and anxiety states. Perhaps fifteen or more are homosexually inclined and another twenty-five depressed. Another hundred may be suffering from so great a feeling of guilt or fear of discovery that their peace of mind and health are jeopardized. The rare individual with complete peace of mind and soul is probably surrounded by those who are carrying several heavy burdens within.

Such a picture of a Sunday morning congregation is not cheerful, but it is so close to the truth that it should make one enter his pulpit with a humble sense of mission. Here are the souls burdened with sin, fearful of life and death, injuring themselves by pride and jealousy, or making life miserable for others through resentments and masked hatred. Here also are the souls who seek forgiveness, a faith to live by, an understanding of themselves to make their living more meaningful, and a basis for good will and sympathy to take the edge off their aggressiveness.

Facing such an opportunity to minister to soul needs, what shall a minister say? Even more important, what shall he refrain from saying? It is well to remember that a sermon may be a soul-injuring instrument as well as a soul-healing force. A sermon may set false goals, stimulate unhealthy resentments, promise a security that is unreal, encourage a submissiveness, on the one hand, or aggressiveness, on the other, that could easily lead to more acute personality difficulties. To be a soul-healing influence, a sermon should face the reality of life honestly, proceed creatively toward goals that are reasonable and challenging to the best in life. It should present a way of living life at its best that is both comprehensible and attainable.

There are certain implicit expressions involved in worship itself that can heal. Quietness, the harmony of music, the majesty of the Scriptures, the beyondness of prayer, the general confession, and words of assurance—all have their function. One woman said to me, "When I leave the church I feel so clean inside." I knew her need and understood what she meant. Worship can do that even without the sermon.

Some ideas and attitudes can be implicit in a sermon. Not every sermon can be about faith, but every sermon can breathe a sense of faith. Not every message can be on the value of the human soul, but every sermon should assume it. Not every homily can deal with problem-solving techniques, but every sermon can assume the presence of a power able to help solve the most serious of human difficulties. Nor can every sermon be theological, but neither should any sermon give a basis for doubt as to the preacher's feeling that God is a real and present force in life.

On the side of the explicit expressions, there is the important function of making the hearer aware of himself as a part of something beyond himself. As Harry Emerson Fosdick says it, he should be led to see himself "not as a part of the problem, but as a part of the solution." Illustrations then become beams of light from a source that can light "every man that cometh into the world." The dead fact becomes alive when teaching becomes the basis for encouragement and insight into life's meaning. Reassurance, as the good news that can fortify the struggling soul, then becomes more than the dangerous and deadening platitude. And the invitation becomes more than a worn-out form, as a chance to add action to assent, toward a goal that is envisioned but not yet achieved.

The tone of preaching becomes different when the preacher pictures himself, first of all, as a minister to souls injured, scarred, or frightened by the experience of life. Even the congregation looks different when no longer seen as a group to judge or applaud the preacher. The preacher then learns that his place is secondary, for people come not to hear him, but to hear God through him. The instrumental nature of his function, when grasped in all its meaning, moves him beyond the unhealthy preoccupation with "What am I going to say?" In its place is the more satisfying contemplation: "To whom shall I be speaking?" "What is his greatest need?" "In the time he gives me, how can I best meet that need?"

In a society where the soul sickness of men and women and children is revealed by increasing divorce rates, juvenile adjustment problems, millions of cases of acute mental illness, and an ever increasing amount of functional illness that reveals the morbid state of the personality, the preacher has a staggering task. Who can begin to evaluate the moral responsibility that rests upon our clergy, to make the opportunity of a hundred thousand sermons each week an actual soul-healing force? When people come asking bread in the form of an understanding of life's meaning, guidance in stress, and insight into the riddles of their own natures, shall they be handed a stone of meaningless exposition or theological abstraction? More than we dare imagine, the answers to such questions may determine the spiritual health of our people for generations to come.

CHAPTER I

Preaching to the Guilt-laden

The minister who lives close to his people is well aware of the effect of guilt on their lives. Sometimes he hears confessions of guilt. More often he sees the behavior which indicates that guilt is at work.

Guilt can be a life-disrupting force. Guilt may so obsess a person that the concept of the self as a creative, forward-moving force is destroyed. It may cause a loss of self-respect or of self-confidence. It may make a person so defensive against imagined suspicion by others that he becomes suspicious of the behavior and motives of those about him. Such suspicion is likely to make him aggressive in his attitude toward others or cause him to withdraw more and more from association with others.

A sense of guilt may easily contaminate interpersonal relations and encourage the very type of behavior that can further increase guilt feelings. Visibly or invisibly, the guilt-saturated personality feels hunted, tortured, and afraid. Often the person develops strange defenses. For instance, the gossip may be a person with guilt feelings who would direct attention to others engaged in the very things he has done or would like to do. The witch-hunter is likely to be suffering from feelings of guilt which he would sublimate or atone for by his exposure of others.

Often guilt feelings are suppressed so that only the careful observer of human behavior can sense the root motives. The person who is always on the defensive may be unconsciously at work to protect himself from exposure. Often those who feel a sense of guilt try to involve others in the same type of behavior that bothers them. This is seen among those who feel uncomfortable about their drinking habits and seek support for their behavior by trying to involve persons whose moral values they envy.

Sometimes the evidences of guilt are found in psychogenic disturbances of the physical organism. A physician once commented about a patient who suffered an onset of severe gastric disturbance after he had cheated a relative out of his portion of an estate: "That man needed a pastor, not a doctor. He was suffering from a guilty conscience." Such effects of guilt may well be unconscious and cannot usually be dealt with until some experience brings them to the level of conscious consideration.

Not all guilt is real guilt. Real guilt, when consciously dealt with, can be corrected by restitution or works worthy of repentance. Unreal or neurotic guilt may have all of the comparable symptoms, with no basis in reality. The emotionally disturbed personality breeds this guilt. It feeds on those stimuli that are often related to religious efforts to "exorcize the devil." It is unfortunate when a soul sorely burdened by neurotic guilt is played on by the preacher who tries to convict his hearers of sin. Like the hypochondriac with a medical book, a person suffering from neurotic guilt may be tragically afflicted by the sin-obsessed preacher.

In preaching there is real danger in confusing the two types of guilt. It is important to understand the difference and to know how the two can be dealt with constructively in preaching. How gently Jesus dealt with those who were burdened by a sense of guilt! How constructively he led them to a new sense of relationship with reality! How slow was our Master to condemn and how quick to encourage the fallen!

19

The preacher must deal with sin as a major guilt-producing factor in life. At the same time he must deal with those persons whose guilt is rooted in a personality disturbance. He cannot serve the Kingdom by adding to unreal guilt; yet he cannot ignore the fact of sin. How then does he proceed in preaching to a congregation where there are both those whose guilt is real and those whose guilt is neurotic and imaginary?

Understanding the problem of the sufferer from neurotic guilt may help the preacher in dealing with it. Edmund Bergler, in his book *The Battle of the Conscience,* indicates the forces at work to disrupt the personality through imagined guilt. He shows how the experiences of childhood may affect future life to the extent that unconscious factors never cease to exert a strong influence. For instance, he indicates how the fear created by a nun in disciplining a little girl in school became a factor so important in her future behavior that it threatened her emotional security and the possibility of a normal, creative marriage relationship. The child repressed the memory of the unhappy experience, but the fears and guilt associated with it became a part of her subconscious response to life situations.

A preacher who would play upon such neurotic guilt could exert a commanding control over such a person. She might be unable to say "no" to any command that had the authority of religion because she could not stand the sense of guilt that would go with such disobedience. But to use such a state of mind and emotion without an awareness of what it would do to the person involved, would be an unwarranted trespassing in the sacred precincts of personality. The only alternative seems to be to preach about guilt in such a way that the person with real guilt will be helped and the person with neurotic or unreal guilt will not be further injured.

Jesus dealt with such disturbed persons calmly and with a

sense of command that minimized the sense of guilt. When others condemned a troubled man, Jesus talked with him as if he were normal. The result was that his life was reorganized about some new feelings and he became "clothed and in his right mind" (R.S.V.). Fosdick preached a sermon on the too sensitive conscience entitled "No Man Need Stay the Way He Is." Instead of condemning those guilty of sins, he gave emotional support to those who had been penalizing themselves because of a false sense of guilt.

Because the preacher in the pulpit can never be aware of all the emotional forces at work in the minds and hearts of his congregation, it is always wise to approach the problem of the guilt-stricken from the positive emphasis on the redeeming love of God, rather than negatively by the threat of punishment. Punishment will come no doubt, but the sufferer from neurotic guilt has already endured more than his misdeeds would warrant. The positive approach that seeks to mediate the redeeming love of God does not injure the person who suffers from unreal guilt, and it does give emotional support to the person with real guilt who can be moved toward restitution. In both instances it can direct the personality toward creative action and more healthy feelings.

The positive approach, concerned with restoring full usefulness in life rather than mere punishment, can recognize the universal nature of sin and the need for confession in order to prepare the mind and heart for forgiveness and the saving power of God's redeeming love. All men stand in need of redemption, so the guilt-stricken may become a member of an inclusive and supporting fellowship in worship rather than a depressed and excluded sufferer.

Bergler indicates that the guilty person may express his feelings through cynicism, hypocrisy and self-derision. He may deride the values that give him a sense of guilt, or he may practice the

21

misuse of values, or he may persist in a type of self-punishment by presenting himself in the worst light possible. It is well to remember that these are the camouflages that guilt may wear. But guilt may also find more positive expression through sublimation, rationalization, tender love, or hard work.

Whenever we preach we can be sure that we are speaking to those who suffer from both types of guilt. How easy it is to say those things that add to the burden of the sufferer from unreal guilt! Probably many such persons identify themselves with the Church as an effort toward restitution. Yet how important it is for us to understand their particular need and to approach it in such a positive way that we will be an instrument for their soul healing, thus preventing further self-condemnation and the rejection of God's redeeming love.

The healthy man strives toward an important, creative purpose in life. The disturbed soul is confused and is likely to think of purposes as defense mechanisms, and defense mechanisms as purposes. The preacher who can so present the healing, redeeming love of God that it becomes the one real goal of life is able to move the guilt-stricken a long step toward more healthful living. The preacher who can make Jesus Christ the friend and guide toward such abundant life gives a positive foundation upon which the guilt-stricken can begin to rebuild life, with new direction and a firm faith in themselves and in God's sustaining love.

Four types of sermons that might be useful in preaching to those who have strong feelings of guilt are indicated in the following résumés.

I

In the first of these sermons the preacher interprets the parable of the Prodigal Son. Without condemnation or judgment, the process of growth from immature and faulty values to sounder judgment is outlined.

RESTORING RIGHT RELATIONSHIPS
Text: *"When he came to himself."*—Luke 15:17

The growth toward mature behavior is not easy for some persons. Some of us learn the hard way and experience is often a rather stern teacher.

With typical adolescent assurance the Prodigal Son rejected the judgments and discipline of his father. Inevitably there comes a time when the growing personality must learn to stand on its own two feet and to develop its own moral judgments. This often involves a time of tension between parents who represent inherited moral values and the youth who is trying to develop his own conscience.

The Prodigal went his way to test the basic values of friendship, money, and ethical patterns of behavior. He used up his inheritance quickly and found that the way he had adopted was far from satisfying. He was now in a position to make contrasts and comparisons.

The Prodigal felt defeated and ashamed, but he had the good judgment to try to do something about it. "When he came to himself," he abandoned the pigsty and started home, resolved to admit his folly and start again on a sounder basis.

Growth toward mature moral values often brings us to a place where we may go to pieces or may "come to ourselves." It is a sign of maturity to learn from experience and to rebuild constructively. The Prodigal handled his sense of guilt and shame creatively. He grew through it. He began to see the importance not only of his own desires but of right relationships to others as well. He accepted the promise of a redeeming love and was restored to life.

In such a sermon the preacher tries to move a person beyond a preoccupation with his guilt feelings to an understanding of how they develop and what can be done constructively to live beyond them. By relating guilt to growth he makes it easier for the hearer to learn the lessons that error can teach, without feeling the necessity for carrying further the sense of guilt that error often leaves.

II

Often the sense of guilt paralyzes the present because of the continual intrusion of the past. In the sermon that follows the effect of guilt is noted by one who carried such a burden, and his prescription for dealing with it is elaborated.

THE POWER OF A NEW BEGINNING
Text: *"Forgetting those things which are behind."*—PHIL. 3:13

Often guilt brings so vivid a memory of the past that the future is paralyzed. Paul knew the nature of such guilt. Had it not been for the urging of Barnabas, he might never have lived beyond it. St. Paul gives a three-point program for moving beyond that type of guilt. Certainly he can speak with authority, for he had on his conscience the vigorous persecution of the early followers of Jesus.

First, he said we should forget the past. This is not easy, but it is easier than allowing the past to ruin the future. It cannot be done merely by saying, "Lo, I will forget." It must involve a discipline of mind that displaces memories of the past with action in the present.

Second, strain forward to what lies ahead. The present can be used to make a more worthy future. What is past is done. We cannot relive it. We can learn from it. It is a sin to fail in present opportunities because a millstone of the past has been tied about our necks. But even straining in the present is of little purpose without a goal.

Third, set a worthy goal. "I press on toward the goal for the prize of the upward call of God in Christ Jesus." (R.S.V.) A purpose that is worthy enough to engage the whole being in creative living leaves little place for remorse, recrimination, or self-deprecation.

The great saints of the church have often been men who found that they could only come to grips with a bad conscience by dedicating themselves to the fulfilling of a high mission in life. They learned from the past but were not enslaved by it. They made the rest of life good for themselves and for others. We share the same privileges.

The effect of such a sermon is to free the guilty person from a crippling burden of guilt. Then the lessons of the past can be learned and acted on, and the opportunities of the future may be accepted with freedom from the severe judgments of the neurotic conscience.

III

In the following sermon the value of confession and the possibility of the use of prayer as a confessional are indicated. Facing the situation that causes guilt helps to remove it, while blind disregard of its existence leaves both the guilt and its effect unresolved.

FACING A SENSE OF GUILT

Text: *"This man went down to his house justified rather than the other."*—LUKE 18:14

According to Jesus there were two guilty men in the story. One was guilty of pride and did not know it. One was guilty of some unspecified sin and knew what to do about it.

The morbid conscience that seeks religious justification for its warped values is not new. We see the personality structure of the Pharisee as he lived then and now.

The true moral conscience is able to face itself and seeks to find justification in the only way it can be found, through right relations with God.

To be emphasized is the idea that a mature conscience is not bound up with a list of things it has not done. Rather, the adjusted adult conscience is able to venture into life with an ability to make judgments, accept risks, make mistakes and seek to correct them.

25

According to this story it is not so much a matter of who is guilty but rather what we choose to be guilty of. The immature are guilty of false standards and never seem to know it. They are in league with evil forces and never sense their relationship. The mature mind inevitably makes mistakes but is able to take the consequences and grow. Humility is essential to growth and to real moral justification.

By indicating that guilt is an inescapable part of human experience, we can bridge the gap between those who feel excluded by guilt and those who do not. Then the guilt-stricken can realize that it is not so much the exceptional nature of their guilt as it is the attitude they have toward it. When this is done they are in a better position to adjust to their feelings and bring their living back toward a more normal range of feelings.

IV

In the following sermon Ralph W. Sockman deals directly with the problem of guilty feelings. He points out that the message of salvation of Christ is made ineffective if the burden of guilt prevents healthful, creative living.

HOW TO BE FREE OF GUILTY FEELINGS [1]
Text: *"I heard thy voice . . . , and I was afraid . . . ; and I hid myself."*—GEN. 3:10

The conscience is the source of our guilty feelings. It acts as a built-in voice of the Creator and not as the echo of the crowd. While it has strong social relationships, it is more than the voice of the crowd. To try to kill the conscience is to try to destroy something sacred to one's own individuality.

To ignore the voice of conscience is to deceive the self, but to become burdened with a sense of unforgivable sin is also to deny the

[1] Adapted from "How to Be Free from Guilty Feelings," *The Upper Room Pulpit*, January, 1951. Used by permission.

nature of Christ's mission. The mission of Christ was to free people
of an unreasonable sense of guilt, for "He shall save his people from
their sins" (Matt. 1:21). Fear is not designed to keep people from
the fruits of salvation but rather to create the concern that can
lead them to it. When the fear becomes more than a concern-cre-
ating agent, it has ceased to serve its function.

The Father loves both the wronged and the wrongdoer. Decency
demands acknowledged guilt, but it would not stop life at that point.
It would use the acknowledgment of a point of guilt as a catalytic
agent to clear the mind and emotions and start the forward motion
of life again. The first steps of Alcoholics Anonymous are a recognition of personal inability to control life, a need for divine help in
bringing life under control, and a willingness to accept such divine
help. It assumes that God knows and understands our feelings and
concerns but would not have us stop there. God's concern is with
fruitful living, and he is anxious to get us on the way toward it. God
can be trusted without reserve. Confess and be free to live creatively
again.

In this sermon Sockman effectively makes one simple point.
Namely: The concern of God is not to fill people with a sense of
guilt, but to use the feeling of guilt as a door of understanding
to open new opportunities for living. So guilt leads to confession,
and confession leads to freedom, and freedom leads to new life,
and God is at work in each step of the way.

CHAPTER II

Preaching to the Sorrow-filled

There is no escaping the prevalence of death. Newspapers and magazines are filled with it. A war-conscious world is always aware of it. Anxious people, in an age of atomic weapons and thermonuclear bombs, can never get sudden death entirely out of their consciousness.

Probably a majority of the persons in any congregation have recently experienced the bereavement of a relative or close friend, and consequently they are giving considerable, if disorganized, thought to the subject. It means that the field is always fertile for a preacher to deal constructively with the problem of sorrow and death.

Military chaplains have indicated that they were asked more questions about death and immortality than about any other subject of a religious nature. Young people in summer camps have in recent years indicated a persistent and deep-rooted interest in this subject that was not shared by their parents a generation ago.

One does not minister very long to people before he realizes the differences in the quality of response to grief situations. Some persons seem to make an easy adjustment to the fact of death and bravely proceed with a deep and sustaining faith. Others seem to be completely disorganized by death and never quite manage to pull the threads of life together again. We find those who are deeply disturbed; but through the slow, healing process of time—or what Joshua Loth Liebman called "sorrow's slow wisdom"—they rebuild their lives on a more secure basis.

Before considering what can be done in preaching to bereaved people it may be well to look at grief and what it does. For the personality involved, grief is a deprivation experience. Something of great personal value is taken away and the sense of loss is acute. If the personality has learned wisely and well the technique for adjustment to deprivation, it has probably developed the resources for meeting grief situations. The early experiences of life may have built up a tolerance to deprivation. When parents try always to give in to a child, they do little to build such a capacity to adjust personal desire to external reality. The mature response to grief is the capacity to accept and adjust to deprivation on a large scale. The emotionally secure individual, who has a sound reality sense, a freedom from guilt feelings, and a healthy capacity to adjust, is usually well able to handle the grief situations of life. The insecure, with limited reality sense and poor adjustment capacity, is severely disrupted by personal loss.

The inadequate personality often reflects this inadequacy in grief situations while it conceals it fairly well under other circumstances. Such grief can disorganize the reasonable responses of persons to life situations. It may make them particularly sensitive to injury or oversight. It may stimulate a marked dependency feeling that may be unwisely expressed. Also, under such conditions, the religious inadequacies of the person may be revealed in a plainer light.

The preacher, in dealing with the sorrow-filled, will realize that his approach is twofold. He must minister directly to the afflicted, and he must carry on a long-range program that will help to undergird the lives of his people for the more adequate handling of such situations as they inevitably develop.

Grief is always related to the personal needs of the grief-stricken. Grief reveals the quality of the emotional life. Grief reveals the level of maturity and the ability to adjust to trying life situations. Feelings of loss and personal loneliness demand adjustment. Displeasure at facing a new set of reality factors demands perspective. Any inner panic at the thought of facing seemingly impossible adjustments merely indicates the quality and intensity of the inner needs.

In such situations it is important to give a measure of emotional support on a temporary basis. Better than empty reassurance is the fact of physical presence. Nothing needs to be said if the understanding and sympathetic presence of a sustaining person exists. This may be true of the quality of pulpit utterance as well as in personal ministrations, for the quality of sympathetic communion may be indicated by the mood rather than by the specific words that are uttered.

An effective preaching program to prepare people for the necessary adjustments of life would have to begin with children. The hush-hush approach to death is false and disruptive. Children are aware of death in all of the rest of nature. If they cannot be trained to handle it on the human level, it will become a source of fear and disturbance. The ability to adjust to small deprivation and temporary loss is the basis on which mature feelings can be built. A strong reality sense becomes the basis for a healthy life, so that religion must be related more to reality than to the mythological and unreal. When real tragedy comes, it is important to have real religion to meet it, not some simulated, mythological framework of false values and unreal premises.

A helpful preaching program would involve at least four major emphases. There would be a full consciousness of the nature of the adjustment involved. There would be an awareness of the resources, personal and spiritual, that are available to help in the adjustment. There would be a real effort to eliminate abstractions and to present suggestions that could open the way to the resources that are available. And not least would be an inspiration that could become the incentive for employing the techniques and resources indicated.

There are some things that the preacher will specifically try to do. He will try to bring comfort through a spiritual orientation of the grief experience. He will try to bring understanding through a rational interpretation of the experience. This can help to remove the basis for bitterness and resentment. It is better to indicate that death is due to an uncontrolled virus than to indicate that in some ways it is God's will, for it is too easy to confuse physical facts with spiritual meanings. The preacher will try to bring new hope to life by encouraging the re-establishment of a continuity to life. Life does not end with bereavement. Often new chapters of heroism and spiritual growth are just about to be written. To do the three things just mentioned, the preacher will seek to undergird the sorrowful person's faith in the basic spiritual nature and meaning of life.

It is probably just as important to indicate what a preacher will not do. He will not give glib assurance that becomes an affront to genuine emotion. He will not give expression to promises that cannot be sustained. He will not ignore the ramifications of the experience in other areas of life. Often the problem of readjustment is not so much a matter of personal emotion as it is a sense of helplessness before economic facts and social responsibility.

The method that the preacher will adopt in proceeding with such matters will depend on the preacher and his established relationship. It is reasonable to assume, however, that the preacher

31

will deal with death and immortality at times other than Easter, when the atmosphere is filled with a festive quality. He might preach on some other subject at Easter time and deal with immortality the following week. He will approach his subject in serious mood, for most people are not prepared or inclined to treat such a topic lightly. He will start with the realities of life, physical or symbolic, and build on them with reasoned clarity. He will approach the subject with the calm assurance that he would use in approaching any other of the great claims of the Christian faith. He would avoid any emotional stimulation because the subject usually carries all of the emotional content needed for most persons. He would avoid all elements of threat in dealing with the subject; for the sensitive eyes of the spirit are not opened to important truths by direct assault, but rather by the winsomeness of understanding, sympathy, and love. To this end, the preacher would try to emphasize the great and sustaining truths of the Christian faith, with a knowledge that they are invisible in nature and with a firm faith in God's goodness as the best guarantee of his sustaining grace even through the trials of death.

The preacher who continually approaches his people with a non-materialistic point of view, and something of what Miguel de Unamuno has called a consciousness of "the tragic sense of life," will find a ready approach to his people. Ian Maclaren, the sensitive Scottish preacher, advised his students to "be kind to everyone, for all are having a hard time." If preaching on the great problems of deprivation and adjustment is effective, it will certainly give a more healthy perspective to those who are faced with the lesser problems of living.

The kind of preaching that can be continually at the task of undergirding life, spiritually and emotionally, gives a background that makes persons adequate for life's bereavement experiences.

Most of us have noticed that those who share in the total program of the church are able to meet such periods of testing with far more strength than those who have no active connection with the church and no regular nourishment for their faith. A sense of purpose for life, a faith in a cosmic plan that sustains the highest aspirations of the spiritual life, a persistent preparation for the concept of life on the spiritual level—these make it possible for such persons to meet crises with adequacy.

The foregoing has been said with the regular preaching service in mind. The funeral service itself presents additional opportunities that have been adequately dealt with by other writers.

A variety of texts and subjects suggest themselves for this type of regular approach to the congregation. The achievement of spiritual insight is suggested by such a text as "This do, and thou shalt live" (Luke 10:28). A consideration of the handling of deprivation might indicate the use of a text like "Not my will, but thine, be done" (Luke 22:42); for then the loss becomes secondary to the spiritual achievement involved. Such a subject as "The Soul's Invincible Surmise" opens the way to an exploration of the ethical, moral, scientific, and theological bases for faith in the immortal life of the human spirit. The basic reality of all life and death is suggested by the words from Joshua, "I am going the way of all the earth" (23:14). The unreasonableness of a fear of death is suggested by the words of the twenty-third psalm, "I will fear no evil." The primacy of life and the tasks of the living are the focus for the words of Jesus, "Let the dead bury their dead" (Matt. 8:22). The feeling of the eternal process of creative human life burdens the words of John the Baptist, "One mightier than I cometh" (Luke 3:16). All of these and many more could become the starting point for helpful sermons on the subject of bereavement and the Christian resources for handling it.

The three treatments of the subject that follow will indicate in more detail how prominent preachers have brought a message of strength and understanding to those who have tasted the experience of death.

I

In the first sermon George A. Buttrick recognizes that the bereaved often respond with a state of depression. This depression can be approached directly by the great affirmations of the faith. Without ignoring the cruel elements in life, he seeks to restore the health of spirit and perspective that can come through balancing that which is lost with what cannot be taken away, the facts of suffering with the fruits of suffering.

THE GREAT ASSURANCE [1]

Text: *"For I am persuaded that neither death, nor life,
. . . shall be able to separate us from the love of God,
which is in Christ Jesus our Lord."*—ROM. 8:38-39

Here is optimism real and rational. Nothing can dam off God's love. Even death only drives a wedge between body and spirit, not between spirit and God.

Paul knew suffering. Yet his suffering led him to faith because he would not let it come between him and God. Sometimes the only way we can plumb the depths of the spirit is to do it with this sense of God's nearness when we need him the most.

Nature is sometimes cruel. Sin takes its toll. But God's love is ever at work to redeem. Mary Magdalene and Matthew illustrate this reedeming force at work on those defeated by life and those threatened by death.

Paul went the whole way, the way of full commitment. Nothing

[1] Adapted from "The Great Assurance" in *The Light Shines Through* (New York and Nashville: Abingdon Press, 1930). Used by permission.

can separate us from God's love when we are willing to make that commitment.

"To love and to cherish until death us do part." Such is the pledge of those who marry. But greater than that is the pledge of God's love, which lives beyond death itself. Our love of God becomes a spiritual investment in the nature of God as revealed in the structure of the universe itself. This exists above and beyond the incidents of life that may seem to cause separation.

One cannot hear such a sermon without moving beyond despair to the higher resolve to create the kind of values in life that death cannot destroy.

II

John Benjamin Magee approaches the problem of bereavement with a concern that all of life be understood as a struggle to achieve spiritual mastery over the accidents of physical existence. He puts Gethsemane and the Cross at the center of this struggle, and the knowledge of the will of God as the goal of it.

THY WILL BE DONE [2]

Text: *"Nevertheless not my will, but thine be done."*—LUKE 22:42

Gethsemane is a geographical place and a spiritual experience. Some would escape it. They only postpone it. Many persons try to avoid it and go on the rocks.

For Jesus, it was a last step in a bitter struggle to reveal God's will to those who would not accept it. The consequence was compromise or a cross.

God is with us in success or failure, in joy or sorrow. His will is found not so much in the material circumstance as in the spiritual quality with which it is met. The law of gravity reveals

[2] Adapted from "Thy Will Be Done" in *The Light Shines Through.* Used by permission.

God's will as well when we rise as when we fall. The wise living of life seeks a recognition of the will of God, first and foremost.

Sometimes the answer to a prayer is less an escape from unpleasant circumstances than the power to see it through—the relation of Gethsemane and the Cross. Sin exacts its toll but we are not bound by it, for God's love is continually at its work of redemption.

Character is built by a demanding discipline. God may help us to gain a noble character, but never by ease and comfort. It is always hammered out on the anvil of cruel experience.

The impact of this sermon should jar persons away from the small personal concerns of their grief and make them face the larger implications of bereavement for the creative mastery of life itself.

III

McIlyar Hamilton Lichliter emphasizes that the body of Christian truth is more than a doctrine. It is a great body of faith built on the belief that God is love.

LOVE LOOKS AT DEATH [3]

Text: *"Jesus saith unto her, thy brother shall rise again.
. . . Whosover liveth and believeth in me shall never
die."*—JOHN 11:23-26

A French peasant who nursed a wounded soldier was given a thousand franc note as a reward. Unaware of its value he framed it to look at the pretty picture on it. We sometimes confuse values. Martha indicated such a confusion when she spoke of her brother rising in the last days. Jesus indicated that his best life, the life of the spirit, was never lost.

The devotee of psychic research tries to communicate with the spirit world. The biologist tries to bring comfort with the idea that

[3] Adapted from "Love Looks at Death" in *The Light Shines Through.* Used by permission.

36

death is a friend. But these approaches do not still the questions in men's hearts. Strong protests arise and we hear the eternal question, "Why?"

Love does more than answer questions. It furnishes feelings of assurance. The by-product of love's protest against death is the hope that makes us strong. The grave could not hold the part of Lazarus that could love. His soul was not restored because, in the first place, it could not be destroyed by death.

Jesus does not offer a doctrine. He offers divine love, the source of the emotional response to life that sees beyond death. For death is nothing but a horizon, and a horizon is nothing but the limit of our vision. Love helps us to see beyond the visible to the unseen and feel the spiritually sustaining force of its counterpart, the love of God.

In this sermon the preacher seeks to involve the bereaved person in a spiritual adventure that can carry him beyond his grief into an understanding of those values that cannot be destroyed. It balances the material and the spiritual and invites the listener to make the choice that is backed by eternal values.

CHAPTER III

Preaching to the Fearful

It is reasonable to assume that each Sunday morning a good portion of the members of any congregation are experiencing the gnawing effects of fear. We live in fearsome times. The times affect the people and they become afraid.

One does not move about in the parish long before he senses the concerns of his people. In one afternoon of calling, the pastor will come upon a variety of fears. Joseph W. is afraid of unemployment. His plant is laying off and his wife and three children need food, clothes, and a home. Willis J. and his wife have a son in the Army in Alaska. He has evidently had a nervous breakdown and they are fearful about his condition. Mary W., a widow with children, has received an eviction notice and is fearful because she has no place to go. William W. has become involved in an "affair" and is beset by fears of discovery and his seeming inability to break it off. Old Mrs. K. knows that she will die before long and she is dreadfully afraid of death.

The pastor realizes that he can probably be most helpful to each of these members of his parish when he talks with them privately. But he also knows that on Sunday morning they will be sitting before him, listening for some word to help allay their fears. Just as surely, he knows that there are others whose fears have not and possibly will not be made known to him. He cannot escape the responsibility to preach to their needs.

How, then, can he best preach to the fearful? What will be the content of his message? What will be the understanding in which it is rooted? What will be his approach so that what he says may be effective?

The pastor's understanding of the nature of fear will direct his preaching approach. He knows that fear, psychologically, has both constructive and destructive possibilities. There is the fear that can lead to deeper understanding and more creative action. In fact, much of mankind's progress has been the result of responses to the fears of starvation, illness, and the effects of the elements. So the wise preacher seeks to conserve the creative possibilities of certain fear situations. He would no more make his message one of empty reassurance that can lead only to despair than he would tell Mary W. not to worry about eviction. Through his sermon he would use the creative possibilities of the emotion, just as he works with Mary W. to use personal and community resources to find her a new home.

The sermon is built on an understanding that fear does things to our bodies, stimulating them to action. The preacher's purpose is to make the action wise and helpful, not only temporarily, but in the long view as well. He tries to direct the constructive potential of the emotional stimulation of fear.

The alternative to constructive use of fear is a deterioration of the emotional state into one of anxiety and impotence in the face of the problem. The glandular stimulation and the muscular conditioning to fear, if oft repeated without creative action toward a solution, will lead to increased nervousness and unreasonable behavior. In war situations this has often been illustrated. Men who were afraid and could act effectively were less inclined to suffer severe emotional disturbances than those whose fear was accompanied by long periods of enforced inactivity. The bodily reaction to fear is to seek safety. The bodily reaction to anger is to take action. When neither safety nor action is possible, fears become cumulative and the impotence of anxiety results.

Since the anxious thrive on sympathy, the preacher will be on guard against the tendency to overpaint the picture of tragedy or catastrophe in life and in the world. As Ruesch and Prestwood have pointed out so well, a calm, objective attitude can be most helpful in directing a person from impotent anxiety to constructive action.[1] Not every sermon can deal with the problem of fear, but every sermon can be rooted in a faith that believes men possess the resources for facing problems. Facing the problems is one long step toward solving them.

But fear is not only a private and personal matter. Increasingly, we are aware of the group factors at work in fear or panic reactions. Faced as we are with world conditions creating anxiety, it is easy to see that panic might be one of the weapons used by those who would seek to bring about the disintegration of morale and the breakdown of group organization. Even now we see the efforts of some who would use fear and its reactions for personal political purposes.

Joost A. M. Meerloo, the Dutch psychiatrist, made extensive studies of the group fear reactions of the Dutch people under the blitz and later made similar studies of the people of some English cities. He found that those who had a strong sense of purpose and a cause could not be easily panicked but that those who had been filled with doubts and fears were more easily brought to the state of disorganized behavior.

Such reactions are a reversion to more primitive types of behavior. We know that, under fear, the lowest forms of life freeze

[1] *Archives of Neurology and Psychiatry*, November, 1949.

into immobility. The oppossum, with its ancient nature, illustrates this behavior. The next stage of reaction is that of flight. Usually it is disorganized and irrational flight. We know the blind fear of a stampede. We also know how a herd of cattle can destroy itself in such flight. At the next level of behavior we have reasoned thought and planned action. Those who are at work with the problems of civilian defense try to establish patterns of behavior to involve many of our citizens in preplanned rational behavior so that they will be kept from the irrational behavior that breeds panic. But the highest and best kind of behavior is that calm, rational, and often self-sacrificial type which grows out of deep faith, sees a purpose, and moves toward it with personal conviction and devotion. This is the sort of thing we mean when we speak of religious devotion.

In times of crisis the pulpit can serve an important function by lifting thought above the level of selfish interest to larger group goals. It can serve to encourage the group attitudes and purposes that will lend stability to group behavior. As cancer represents primitive tissue run wild, so panic represents primitive group emotions run wild. Through the alerted pulpit the church can be continually at the task of clearing away the primitive emotional reactions that build up a cumulative loss of tolerance to crisis situations.

When those rise among us who, for personal and selfish purposes, try to play upon the fears of our people, it is the pulpit's task to restore clarity of vision and perspective to group relationships. The slow paralysis of group fear is a first long step toward the condition wherein panic can breed. A popular writer not long ago wrote a book on the subject *How to Stop Worrying and Start Living*. It might well be reversed, *How to Start Worrying or Stop Living*. In a very real sense, unless there is a marked concern for the type of fear reaction that is being generated by self-seeking individuals, there may well be a mood created that will make careful, rational action in a crisis practically impossible. The pulpit, with its authority and its grip on eternal values, can be continually at the task of calling people back to the habits of thought and patterns of action that can best guarantee reasonable and constructive behavior under those conditions that breed personal fears and group reactions.

The sermon that ministers to the fearful listener is based on a deeper understanding of his fear and its implications than the listener himself possesses. It refuses to do for him some things that he might want. It refuses to give empty reassurance, meaningless sympathy, and an overdrawn picture of the problems which the hearers face. Rather, it encourages a calm appraisal of the problem that causes the fear, an objective evaluation of the resources available to meet it, as well as a stimulus or inspiration to use the resources effectively.

I

The first of the four sermon outlines that we will look at in relation to the needs of and approach to the fearful, uses the graphic narrative material that the Old Testament abundantly affords. The well known story of David and Goliath is symbolic in nature. Goliath represents the large problem that is the source of the fears. The listener may come to identify himself with David, who overcomes the problem.

ARMOR AGAINST FEAR

Text: *Narrative of David and his combat with Goliath*—I SAM. 17

The first point to emphasize is that David was determined to be himself and to use the resources he had developed. He wanted no part of Saul's armor or sword. It was not a part of himself. He properly evaluated himself in terms of the problem he faced.

Second, he refused to be cowed by irrelevant circumstances. Saul doubted him, his brothers cautioned him, Goliath berated and threatened him. But that was all secondary to the main issue. David properly assayed the situation and his relation to it.

Third, David proceeded upon a religious assumption, that a person who does his best to know and do God's will is sustained by a cosmic support that adds to his strength, makes stable his assurance, and increases his chance of success.

This outline suggests a useful approach to the fearful at these points. It does not minimize the problem. It gives no false assurances. It stimulates the individual to be himself and to use his own resources. Similarly, it shows the importance of keeping one's eyes on the main problem, rather than allowing strength to be sapped by all sorts of subsidiary fears and doubts. Finally, it emphasizes the constructive use of religious faith, not as a guarantee of easy success but as the stimulus to bring out the best within the person.

II

A New Testament approach to the same theme is suggested by the words of II Timothy.

POWER OVER YOUR FEARS

Text: *"God hath not given us the spirit of fear; but of power, and of love, and of a sound mind."*—II Tim. 1:7

Here the religious assurance opens the way to action on three levels. First is the assurance of power. This is commonly assumed to be physical. The very fact of fear is often overcome as soon as physical action is taken to move beyond the fear-creating situation.

Second is the spiritual resource of love. Many fear-generating situations are the result of the breakdown of love, patience, understanding, and good will. The fears of children, employees, citizens, may obviously stem from a breakdown of the concept of love in human

43

relations. God is love and God's nature at work in human relations resolves the conflicts that may create fear.

Third is the matter of ability to think clearly. Many fears can be removed by a careful and constructive analysis. Instead of agitated emotions, the use of calm reason and intelligent evaluations is of real importance in meeting fears.

This approach, naturally less graphic and narrative, has its value in emphasizing the variety of religious resources available for meeting our fears. They may be met through constructive physical action, well directed emotional insight, or the use of sound reason. The religious inspiration is implicit, for God is not in the fears but rather in the resources that can overcome the injurious nature of the fears.

III

Another approach might be designated as the psychological. Here a number of text and biblical settings would suggest themselves. The main purpose would be to aid the hearer to see himself in relation to his problem.

TOWARD AN UNDERSTANDING OF FEAR
Text: *"There were they in great fear, where no fear was."*
—Ps. 53:5

First, the preacher might show how fear grows, how it manifests itself, and how it affects life—biologically, psychologically, and socially.

Second, he would show how faith in one's self, in other people, and in God can make it difficult for fear to possess a person; for "perfect love casteth out fear." Faith can be used as the opposite of fear. The effects of faith on the person can be illustrated biologically, psychologically, and socially.

Third, the function of religion is to offer insight into the nature of the problem and the nature of the person who has the problem, as well as to make available the resources for solution. Often, insight into the self is a primary requisite in handling destructive fears.

The preacher who is interested in assisting the frightened souls in his congregation may flavor all of his utterance with the understanding of the needs of those suffering from this particular emotional disturbance. But he can surely give special thought to the problem, both individually and socially, by an occasional use of the biographical-narrative, the theological, or the psychological approach, as his own interests and inclination may indicate. In our day we cannot be unaware of the persistent, gnawing effects of fears that may grow into the major emotional disturbances which cripple the human soul irreparably. The preacher, week in and week out, may serve a useful and valued function in understanding the fearful and in helping them direct their fear-inspired resources constructively.

IV

In the following sermon Robert J. McCracken gives a specific program for dealing with the fears that beset life. Aware of both psychological need and the spirit's resources, he faces the problem without subterfuge and seeks to release the sources of personal strength that can deal wisely with fear.

WHAT TO DO WITH OUR FEARS [2]

Text: "What time I am afraid I will trust in [the Lord]."—Ps. 56:3

These are the days of great fears. Some seem to be borne inwardly, others outwardly. There appears to be no end to fear-breeding experiences.

J. A. Hadfield, a Harley Street specialist on emotional disorders, says that the treatment of the shell-shocked demands that they try

[2] Adapted from "What to Do with Our Fears," *The Upper Room Pulpit*, May, 1950. Used by permission.

to recall and face their fears rather than repress and forget them. It is not weakness but wisdom to admit and face one's fears. A four-point program for dealing with fears is suggested.

1. Admit and face one's fears.

2. Recognize that self-interest breeds fears, and concern for others dissolves them. The compassion of Jesus continually kept him living beyond his fears.

3. Pray about your fears by name and in mentioning them you will find the courage to face them and the rest of life.

4. Remember that we are in God's hands and that his faith can overcome our fears. The fact that we are not alone in facing our fears reassures us.

Eternal love is a major asset in dealing with the fears that disrupt life.

The value of this sermon is not only in its truly religious orientation but in the practical suggestions that relate to the naming, facing, and dealing with specific fears. The simple fear is easier to handle than the unspecified anxiety that it may create. So start handling fears at the level where they *can* be handled and realize the religious resources that are available to help you in doing it. Such a direct message from the pulpit may prevent the more damaging effects of fear.

CHAPTER IV

Preaching to Those Bothered by Alcohol

The consequences of the use of alcohol for beverage purposes present one of the major personal and social problems of our day. It is a problem that must be recognized by the pulpit; however, it is one that is difficult to handle. In the first place, those whom we would be most anxious to reach are not usually in the congregation. In the second place, an increasing number of church people indulge, and a vigorous pulpit utterance on the subject is considered to be an unreasonable and intemperate judgment of their practice.

Having recognized these difficulties, we are obliged to define more clearly the nature and direction of our message. Alcohol presents a problem which, directly and indirectly, bothers many people—morally, socially, economically, and emotionally. A wise approach to the problem may help to solve it. An unwise approach may increase the needs that alcohol satisfies.

An English study of the needs and satisfactions related to the use of alcohol equated these needs with basic religious concerns. The personality faced with the problems of life needs reassurance, a means for breaking down artificial barriers, a way of releasing tension, and a measure of self-esteem. Alcohol furnishes these on a temporary basis, while religion gives them on a permanent basis. Alcohol is a false substitute; for it has a reaction that

47

diminishes self-esteem, creates more tension, sets up new barriers, and gives false reassurance. But the interesting conclusion of the study indicates that the needs of the alcohol-user are essentially the same as those of the deeply religious person. His quest, however, has led him toward a false answer to his problems. He is often able to respond to the claims of a religious faith and to find the true answer to his needs, if the claims of faith are presented with understanding and conviction.

The pulpit has a responsibility to those who feel such needs and seek such satisfactions. It also has a responsibility to increase the understanding of those whose more stable adjustment to life makes it difficult for them to deal with and understand the plight of the person for whom alcohol has become a problem. We are more likely to have an opportunity of preaching to those concerned about the drinking habits of others than to those who are faced with the problem themselves.

In our preaching it is also important to make some rather clear distinctions. Among those who drink there are three classes. First are the social drinkers for whom alcohol presents no present problem. They can drink or not as it pleases them. They are usually sensitive to any word implying that there is danger of their developing a problem with their drinking. Then there are the problem drinkers, who are aware of the effect of drink upon their habits, their behavior, and their relations to others. They often try to cover up their problem but are aware of its effects. They need help and often want it. The third group includes those who have a strong and uncontrollable compulsion to drink —the alcoholics. They have a problem but are not likely to care so long as they can get enough to drink. This group, in need of special help, usually fight against it until they are at the end of their human resources.

Among those who do not drink there seem to be three groups

also. First, there are those who avoid the problem and all who are related to it as much as possible. Then there are those who, by their attitude and behavior, tend to drive others to drink. Also there are those who take a healthy and constructive attitude toward the needs of others who face a drinking problem. Often those who drive others to drink are suffering from many of the same emotional problems that the drinker seeks to satisfy with alcohol, plus a moral rigidity and emotional intolerance that makes them difficult to live with. Preaching may help to bring them to a measure of understanding and may give some guidance to them in dealing with their own problems as well as the problems of others. In every parish a solid core of healthy-minded people are continually at work, with patience and understanding, to help the drinker with his problems. The pulpit can confirm and encourage them at their task.

In order to be of help it is important to present the problem of the alcoholic or the problem drinker for what it is, a symptom of and a capitulation to immature feelings, often rooted in the subconscious. We do not need to accept the full implications of psychoanalytic theory to sense the cogency of its view that dependency on alcohol is a reversion to early childhood techniques for adjusting to discomfort by shoving something into the mouth. The drinker is one who wants to escape an unpleasant reality. It may be as mild as a troublesome shyness or as severe as a deep and unresolved hostility, but the technique of escape is the same; namely, take a drink and short circuit the portion of the brain that is aware of the problem.

Some persons drink to destroy themselves, employing much the same dynamics as the suicide would use except that the effect is partial. Some turn their aggressive impulse against others to make life miserable for those they love and hate at the same time. Often the drinker has emotional problems related to sex.

49

Some studies have indicated a significant correlation between problem drinkers and latent homosexuals. Alcohol releases the drinker from those fears and inhibitions related to his sexual behavior. In a sense he is trying to heal a psychic disturbance with alcohol as his self-administered psychotherapy.

The drinker may be troubled by guilt or grief. Often the drinker is filled with remorse and, in his effort to escape, only increases that remorse. Certainly, to preach to him in scolding terms would only increase the problem that, with his weakened spiritual resources, is already too much for him to handle. Alcoholics Anonymous has found that the disturbed drinker responds more readily to kindness, understanding, and sympathy than he does to preaching and scolding.

The concern of the nondrinker may well be to help the drinker build up his inner strength so that he can begin to live with himself and his problems rather than try to escape from them. The non-drinker should seek to understand enough about the state of mind of the drinker—before, during, and after a drinking episode —so that the person can be dealt with helpfully rather than hindered. The drinker's task is to gain the inner strength needed to face reality and to recognize that he is the central problem in that reality.

In speaking to the drinker himself, it is well to remember that certain things must not be done. The moralistic approach does not help in most cases, for the drinker is already more thoroughly acquainted with the threatening aspect of his behavior than anyone else. He wants more strength, not more scolding. Also it is important to avoid the shallow analysis of the problem, with an easy approach to its solution. To tell him that all he needs is the strength to say the little word "no" is to indicate that you do not understand what he is fighting. To tell him that all he needs is muscle control—enough to let go of the glass—is no help. He knows it is not an honest or realistic approach to the problem that is shattering him inside. Also, it is important to avoid the dramatic or melodramatic descriptions of the alcoholic's behavior which merely add to his sense of guilt. He is already guilty "nigh unto death." I know of one drinker who was urged to hear an evangelist who preached a bloodcurdling sermon on "demon rum." The man went to listen and came home to hang himself. He was plunged into the depths of depression by the sense of guilt he could not bear. The sermon was good entertainment for those who were not faced with the drinker's problem, but it came close to being murderous cruelty for the afflicted drinker himself.

The more positive possibilities that are both helpful to the drinker, and to those who would help him, call for an emphasis on understanding the conditions that create the problem and the forces that can work for its solution. The drinker needs to know why he drinks in order to grasp how not to drink. Most persons for whom alcohol has become a problem do not enjoy drinking, but they feel unable to cope with a drive that in many instances becomes compulsive. The more they are involved in an escape technique, the less are they able to face the causes for their emotional turmoil. Again and again, those who have gained control over their compulsive behavior indicate two things. First, they found some person who was willing to help them face themselves, and then they found a power from God that helped them to do something about the self they had finally faced. The preacher can be guided at this point by a method that has been helpful so many times in groups such as AA. A person cannot deal with a self he not only does not know, but is continually seeking to escape. He needs help to stop and do a rightabout-face, look at himself honestly, and ask the help of God to deal with this ugly thing he finally recognizes as the self that is, but need not be.

Sermons may come at the problem from many angles. The

social approach may deal with prevention and the removal of causes. The psychological approach may indicate the disturbances within the personality that cause one to seek escape and may point out the positive forces at work to integrate the person at a more mature level. But the religious approach is the one that is able to add power to understanding. One of the problems of the drinker is his impotent insight. He knows but cannot do, or at least he cannot do when he is dependent upon his own strength alone. The religious emphasis on a redeeming love is able to relieve the pressures of burdensome guilt and free the soul for more constructive uses of its strength.

Religious faith has about it the sustaining quality for life that can help a person fix his eyes on a goal and move toward it through temptation, pressure, discouragement, and failure. Not every drinker solves his problem at the first attempt. He needs his faith and purpose restored. The understanding friend in the pulpit who preaches the power of a positive faith may be ministering to the needs of the drinker even when he is dealing with subjects unrelated to the specific area of alcohol. When he helps to build a creative understanding of the self, he is increasing the power to control the self. When he preaches a positive faith that comes from God's redeeming love, he is helping to mediate the power that can sustain the person involved in a fight to control himself.

Imagination is often needed to get past the guard that moderns put up around their indulgences. One minister preached a sermon on the problem of alcohol and never once mentioned the word. He started by talking of the sacred cows of India. He described the irrational behavior related to the worship of sacred cows. He told how these sacred cows roamed at will, destroying produce, property, and people, no effort being made to have them serve a useful purpose. While people suffered and children died for want of milk, these cows were not eaten nor were they bred for milking purposes. Such irrational behavior violates basic human values and operates against the standards of Christian society.

When the picture had been painted so that there seemed to be thorough agreement as to its folly, the preacher shifted to the question. What about *our* sacred cow? Then for the rest of the sermon he talked about the attitude of many who try to protect the sacred cow that stalks our highways, invades our homes, disrupts family life, takes milk from children, denies food to adults, disrupts economic activity, and, generally speaking, brings havoc to the lives of millions of people. He spoke of the places of worship set up on nearly every street corner for people to pay their homage to this sacred cow. He told how the worship of this sacred cow had become so dominant in American life that four dollars were spent in its support for every dollar spent on education, and eight times as much as for all the religious enterprises of the country. Without mentioning the word "alcohol" he built up a picture of irrational attitudes and behavior that was more convincing than a frontal attack could have been. It was particularly fitted to the mood of those who become restless at any direct temperance sermon but who need, more than others, to see the effects of alcohol in their proper light.

The three sermon résumés that follow indicate how the subject of alcohol and its related problems has been dealt with in three different ways.

I

Recognizing that, for many, the dependence upon alcohol is a substitute for the values of religion, the preacher, in the following sermon, develops the character of such inadequate religion as compared with the essentials of the Christian faith. Without dwelling on alcohol, the preacher may use it as an illustration and, in the process, raise important questions as to the nature of dependence on such a form of self-applied psychotherapy.

THE POWER OF GOD

Text: *"O ye of little faith. . . . Seek not ye what ye shall eat, or what ye shall drink, neither be ye of doubtful mind."*—LUKE 12:29

Jesus had been talking of the importance of life. He tried to help his hearers put things into their proper relationships. Persons of small faith seek after small things—food, drink, clothes—and in so doing they miss life's meaning. Those who put God first find all that is needed to sustain life's important purposes.

Small faith indicates an inadequate concept of God. The person with a false god operates on the basis of his small faith, and life shows the consequences.

Small faith indicates an inadequate concept of others. The person with false ideas of human relationships disrupts social life and brings misery to himself and others. His small faith in people is reflected in all his dealings with them.

Small faith is rooted in an inadequate view of self. Low self-esteem, a sense of inferiority, a practice of self-rejection—these destroy the initiative and limit the use of the talents available. Such feelings indicate a talent-burying trait.

The antidote to this small faith is an adequate concept of God and the meaning of the creator-creature relationship. Seek first the kingdom of God and his righteousness and all these other things shall be added to you.

While such a sermon makes no attempt at a frontal attack on the dependence on alcohol, it does seek to raise the questions that need to be asked by one who is concerned about his behavior and is seeking to find the resources to grow beyond it.

II

This sermon is directed toward those who would like to escape any responsibility for the drinking behavior of relatives or friends. Without dwelling specifically on the problem of drink, the sermon can be used to show the indivisible nature of the forces at work to relate the drinker to the nondrinker.

SOCIAL RESPONSIBILITY

Text: *"Am I my brother's keeper?"*—GEN. 4:9

First, the murderer's question "Am I my brother's keeper?" is placed in its context.

Social responsibility is a matter of self-protection. The interests of the individual are threatened by the disintegration of the community. Interrelationship is inevitable. No one can wash his hands of this interdependence.

Social responsibility is a matter of mature judgment. The idea developed by Harry A. Overstreet in *The Great Enterprise* indicates the need for such maturity and responsibility for the growth and development of a better society.

Social responsibility is a matter of religious fulfillment. It is not a matter of choice, but of God's command. As injury to one is injury to all, so also the growth of spiritual resources for one increases the benefits for all.

The mature Christian cannot and should not seek to escape the responsibility for his behavior, example, attitudes, or representative capacity. If self-indulgence destroys, then the mature Christian makes no place in his life for such self-indulgence.

The effect of such a sermon should be to encourage a re-examination of the attitude of the listener toward his own behavior, as it is seen by others and as it affects his concern for the welfare of those who may be struggling against odds that seem too great for them to handle by themselves.

III

Alcoholics Anonymous uses a religious resource when it acknowledges man's inadequacy to cope with his problem and the need to recognize dependence on God for self-mastery. Put into the traditional religious framework, this sermon tries to do the same thing.

INNER STRENGTH FOR LIFE

Text: *"Cast thy burden upon the Lord, and he shall sustain thee."*—Ps. 55:22

There is a cumulative effect of worry and overwork.

There is need for creative release from life's tensions. This is found in an ability to live one day at a time—free of yesterday, unburdened by tomorrow, filled with assurance for today.

There is a source of creative release. There is a relaxation that truly relaxes. Often the fatigue of the spirit is ignored though the need for spiritual refreshment and strength is of primary importance.

There is a technique of creative release. There are ways to find peace of mind and relaxation of spirit that leave no unpleasant aftereffects. There are resources in private worship that can be developed to the point where they sustain life. There are values in group worship that strengthen the person for whatever life may bring.

In communion with God, and the faith that is its product, a person finds the sustaining power of real inner serenity.

The drinker seeks release that usually tends to be destructive of his human relations and his personal values. The aim of this sermon is to point the way toward a type of release from life's problems that is positive and creative. It does not dwell on a dependence on alcohol to the exclusion of other types of negative release, but it does relate such a dependence, through illustration, so that it can be seen and evaluated for what it is.

CHAPTER V

Preaching to the Insecure

Here we are dealing with one of the less clearly defined needs. The elements that lead to insecurity are many, and the devices used as a protection against the effects of insecurity are so numerous that we need not be too concerned about overlooking *somebody* as in overlooking some *aspect* of the subject. Here, as elsewhere in preaching to human needs, we can be sure that needs come in groups and that the tense, the insecure, and the person bothered by alcohol may be one and the same; our preaching in these three areas may in effect be but three different lines of approach to the problems of the same person.

Nearly everyone in our day feels insecure. Many do not admit it. Even when admitted and faced, it is not always possible for a person to control this feeling. While doing some special work for the Air Force, I was made aware of the fine spirit of those who carry a heavy burden of defense work as jet pilots. In talking with them and watching them on duty, I was impressed by the way they work strenuously to keep mind and body always alert and sensitive. A man cannot operate planes at five or six hundred miles per hour and allow himself to become dull. While the attitude of the jet pilots represents a fine spirit of self-discipline, it is also one of the useful devices employed to keep a deep inner feeling of uncertainty and insecurity under control.

Yet the flight surgeon reported that even this strenuous discipline cannot keep their inner organs from showing signs of strain, as the large amount of gastrointestinal disturbance among the pilots testifies.

The unstable society in which we live breeds instability in persons, homes, business, and community. Persons find difficulty in planning for their futures, and uncertainty becomes a part of their approach to life situations. Homes are made insecure by many moves, numerous new adjustments, the breakup of the old ties and dependable relationships, and the types of separation that military service demands. Business ventures are not easily supported because of rapid changes in methods and techniques, and all of these factors affect the quality of community life, where uncertainty breeds confusion and confusion stimulates insecurity.

The Church has a mission and an answer in these times of insecurity. It was born in such days and has made its most effective ministry during such periods in history. But the Church's answer should not add more confusion to the picture by calling the insecure "secure." Isaiah long ago pointed out the dangers of calling the good evil and the evil good. Nor is it the Church's function to give aspirin for malignancy and sprinkle rosewater on the deep wounds of the insecure. Issues are not solved by avoiding them or by trying to make them seem to be something they are not. Rather, the function of the Church and the pulpit is to help the insecure to see the cause of their uncertainty and confusion where they do not see it, and to help them deal with it constructively where and when they do.

In a mature view of life, security is found in an acceptance of reality. Jesus, in speaking to his followers, indicated that this reality acceptance must take place at three levels. There is the acceptance of self, which is basic to any acceptance of the reality about us. The insecure person who spends his time fooling himself and living in a variety of dream relations within himself is certainly in no position to develop a reality sense in relation to others or to God. But these reality acceptances are all interrelated. There is also the important matter of the neighbor—the acceptance of others, free from artificial barriers or false standards. Much insecurity in human relations develops at the point of these barriers and false standards. If a person cannot see himself as he is or human relations as they are, it is quite certain that he will not be able to establish a sustaining reality relationship with God, who demands a wholeness of response to him. Quoting Deuteronomy 6:5, Jesus put this matter of relationship at the three levels: "Thou shalt love the Lord thy God with all thy heart, and with all thy soul, and with all thy strength, and with all thy mind; and thy neighbour as thyself" (Luke 10:27). This is reality acceptance at its best.

Most of the insecure are not able to function effectively at these three levels. How then can they be helped to approach their problem constructively? It would seem that the function of the preacher is twofold. First, he must evaluate the dependence on inadequate forces that leads to insecurity. Second, he must enunciate the values that make for security and indicate how they may be acquired.

The three great enemies of inner security are materialism, infantilism, and escapism. Each of these may be dealt with by the preacher in the context of traditional pulpit utterance.

Jesus portrayed the inadequacy of the approach to life which builds larger and larger barns for material possessions but fails to make provision for the spiritual life. Yet the evaluation of life and human achievement largely by material standards, remains the great curse of our age. Many of those who worship with us on a Sunday morning are sensing a frustration and futility that stems from too great a dependance on material things. Such dependence inverts the process of achieving sustaining values. All the material possessions cannot add one cubit to spiritual stature, but real spiritual growth can lend meaning to all the rest of life and bring to material possessions a new value as they serve spiritually-motivated living.

The preacher in our day has a dual responsibility in regard to this matter of materialism. He must continually indicate the inadequacy of material standards for life judgments. He must indicate the various dangers to life that develop when material standards become the determinants of behavior and life values. He must indicate the subtle disguises that such standards wear as they relate even to the religious practices of the community, for the pride and satisfactions that come with material achievement may often obscure the values that derive from a true sense of human worth and spiritual obligation.

But the preacher must not be content with indicating a negative attitude toward the dangers of materialism as he sees it all about him. His task calls for more than diagnosis and description. He must indicate the winsomeness of spiritual values that can supplant mere material standards of judgment. He must place the needs of the soul in such clear light that men will readily know that they cannot be satisfied apart from the values that take account of the soul. Many persons feel the inadequacy of their materialistic culture but have never had a commanding alternative presented in such a way as to win their loyalty. Though much of personal and social ill comes from materialism, it is equally true that spiritual values do not come easily or automatically. They must be presented persistently as a challenging alternative to the demands of materialism. This is well within the central stream of the preacher's obligation. For who has a greater responsibility for pointing out the spiritual nature of man's creation and the important sense of relationship that his creation gives him with the source of all spiritual values, God himself?

The nature of our society is such that physical maturity is reached long before there is a comparable maturing of the social, emotional, and economic status. This means that the delayed maturing involved in delayed responsibility often leaves elements of immaturity that affect later life. Immaturity may show itself in an overdependent attitude, often directed toward the church and the minister. Or it may be evidenced by irresponsibility in relation to family, social behavior, or personal habits. Because it represents such a significant area of concern, a special chapter will be required for its consideration. But it is important to mention in passing that the immature are invariably insecure and their response to preaching is often readily discernible. The preacher should guard against any temptation to take advantage of such dependency; rather than cater to such immature manifestations he should try to help his listeners to accept responsibility for their choices and behavior.

The insecure often build about themselves a structure of escape techniques. These, they feel, are an adequate protection against the cruel realities of existence. Yet the tragedy is that often these defenses shut them off from the best part of life itself. The "escape artist" usually has a variety of protections against seeing himself as he is. He is the one who has difficulty in applying a sermon to himself but is always willing to concede that those who should have heard it were not there. He is quick to blame others for matters for which he is responsible. He is anxious for approval but falls short of the behavior that warrants it; then he claims that others take advantage of him. In short, his defenses are always standing in the way of achievement; yet he either does not wish, or does not know how, to move beyond them.

Recognizing that true religion demands the finest devotion of

61

mature persons, the preacher continually holds up standards of mature behavior. He does not allow himself to overplay a sentimental dependence on miraculous techniques to achieve those things that may better be the result of a healthy cause-effect relationship. He may well point out how each of the temptations of Jesus was to an immature use of power, but that the Master accepted the responsibility of maturity and would not escape the demands of a cause-effect relationship in proving his sonship. In this way the pulpit can withhold the emotional support that reinforces crippling escape devices and can throw the listener more and more upon his own resources in meeting life squarely.

In the process of enunciating the positive forces that make for security, the sermon may well be the instrument for increasing genuine spiritual insight. The work of the psychoanalyst verifies the fact that spiritual security is a personal achievement in co-operation with some other person. One psychiatrist has reported that though he himself does not pretend to be a religious man, he cannot help being impressed by the fact that, in twenty-five years of active practice in New York City, he has never had a patient who really knew how to pray. Perhaps it is too much of a simplification to say that when people in general knew the practice of prayer there were no psychiatrists, and when they rather generally lost the art of active communication with that "Other," they fell prey to the spiritual insecurities that made the psychiatrist a necessary substitute.

But just as the psychotherapist seeks to lead his patient beyond a dependence upon escapes to a realistic view of himself, so the pulpit must move beyond a reliance on shallow reassurance. No physician of the emotions would feel that supplying a patient with rose-colored glasses would really solve the person's problem. Nor should the sermon be guilty of supplying rose-colored glasses instead of a strengthened reality sense. The sermon that declares, "Everything will be all right if you only believe," is indicating only a small portion of the truth. What you believe is never a generalization or an abstraction, if spiritual security is to be achieved. Rather it is a premise that becomes a basis for action. False beliefs that reinforce a faulty reality sense serve only to increase the threat of that type of action that can further disrupt the personality.

William H. is considered to be deeply religious though one does not need much insight to sense the superficial nature of his belief. He reads enough books of daily devotions to sustain a small parish. He devours books and magazines on faith healing. He reads every book published which has to do with the mysterious powers that come through certain types of positive thought. Yet he has not done a day's work in eight years though there is little evidence of any real physical malady. He is content to let his wife work and support him. He enjoys sermons of inspiration and those that deal with psychological insight. He will testify at informal midweek services concerning the saving grace of God that has kept him going from day to day in spite of "severe physical handicaps." But when it comes to any positive action, he has developed a variety of techniques for avoiding it. He probably understands more about spiritual and psychological dynamics than any other person in the parish, but it is an impotent insight.

While it is probably too much to expect that preaching will break through defenses so solidly built, it is certainly reasonable to feel that preaching should not reinforce the false reality sense that is disrupting the life of William H. and others who are more or less like him. He should rather be encouraged to grow up and accept an adult's responsibility. He should be obliged to face himself as he is, an adept escape artist using his mind and its control over his body to escape adult responsibilities. He should be encouraged to accept the reality of whatever handicaps may be his and come to grips with them like a man. Only then will he move beyond the stage where his religion is a part of a pattern of escape, to the place where his religion is a force for self-understanding and the facing of reality.

When insecurity is seen to be not so much economic as it is spiritual, not so much social as it is a personal inadequacy in the acceptance of others, not so much a matter of cosmic catastrophe as it is an inability to accept and adjust to God's law as revealed in the structure of the universe, then the way is clear for the preacher to deal more constructively with the problems of the insecure people who sit before him on a Sunday morning. The following sermon résumés will be helpful in indicating such an approach to the needs of the insecure.

I

Often insecurity comes through an inversion of the basic values of relationship to God and the universe. Immature and insecure persons act as if they were saying, "What do I require of the Lord?" The following sermon tries to set this matter right by indicating that God makes the ultimate demands and that man fulfills them only when his beliefs result in a series of actions and relationships that show an ability to face himself realistically and to subject his life to a Power beyond.

WHAT DOTH THE LORD REQUIRE?

Text: *"What doth the Lord require of thee, but to do justly, and to love mercy, and to walk humbly with thy God?"*—Mic. 6:8

Life gains stature and direction when it is governed by the requirements of God and his reality rather than the disruptive satisfactions of self-interest and self-indulgence. A neurosis has been defined as a false religion, where the center of worship is the self and self-will. Conversely, then, true religion and the healthful life is dominated by a search for God's will and by the behavior that results from seeking to implement that will.

To do justly is the first requirement. Justice is the basis of right relations with others. It can weigh the interests of others as well as self and arrive at objective conclusions. Justice is a constituent of love, for there can be no true love without justice and no true justice without some of the elements of love.

To love mercy is to go a step beyond justice. Mercy adds the quality of emotional response and understanding to the reasoned judgments of pure justice. To be strictly just, according to any established code of laws, does not fulfill all of the requirements of right relationship with others. The feelings are so important to life that they cannot be ignored in human relations. Mercy involves the fine art of empathy—being willing and able to put one's self in the place of another and feel his feelings with him.

To walk humbly with God is the premise upon which justice and mercy rest, for humility is an essential quality of the learning process. If we would learn about ourselves and our behavior we must be able to see ourselves without false pride. If we are to learn about others we must see them without arrogance. Both areas of right relationship become possible when we are able to subject our small world of values to that larger structure of law and order and love that is revealed in the nature of God.

Such a sermon forces the listener to consider objectively the basic premises of his relationship to others. It may cause him to reassess the values upon which he operates and to subject them to a critical evaluation that is beyond the crippling area of small self-interest and closer to the healthful area of God-centered living.

II

There is a measure of reasonable adult dependence which, discovered, brings security to life. The ability to look at the universe as friendly toward the values that man cherishes is essential to mature faith. Man need not feel that "the things we care for most are at the mercy of the things we care for least." [1] Preaching may well use every opportunity to reinforce this mature and dependable faith as essential to emotional security. The following sermon résumé indicates one way of doing it.

I SHALL NOT WANT

Text: "The Lord is my shepherd; I shall not want."—Ps. 23:1

Our wants are determined as much by our values as by our needs. Needs vary as our values change. So-called "needs" are far more numerous today than they were a generation ago because our standards of living have changed. A similar relationship can also be true with our spiritual needs. The Psalmist looked at the security of the sheep and anaylzed the factors of his own dependency relationship. At every point—food, shelter, security, and care—the shepherd made adequate provision and the sheep were satisfied. The Psalmist looked toward God for a similar relationship, regarding him as the source of the values that determined his own consciousness of need.

Fact vs. Fiction. We move a long step toward security when we are able to separate our true needs from our false desires. We waste much life and energy seeking what is futile, whereas an investment of self in God's will so clarifies our values that often those things which once seemed essential are no longer even desirable.

Incidents vs. Insights. Much that happens in life can be handled more adequately if we see it in context. Little things do not seem so disturbing nor larger happenings so catastrophic if they are seen as incidents in a larger pattern of life. That insight which can help us to "see life and see it whole" can turn many of our experiences of spiritual want into moments of spiritual opportunity.

Faith vs. Fears. This attitude is especially effective when we have

[1] W. P. Montague, Belief Unbound (New Haven: Yale University Press, 1930.)

a faith large enough to keep our fears under control. The Psalmist does not indicate that, to keep it a satisfying experience, all of life must be "green pastures." He is equally aware of "the valley of the shadow of death," but for him it is not evil. Rather, it is a part of a plan that affirms God's regnant nature. When his faith is well established, his fears diminish. Many of our wants are directly related to our fears—the fears of false pride, the fears of insecurity, the fears of death. But these become incidental to a larger pattern when one is able to relax in adult dependency, sure that "underneath are the everlasting arms."

In this sermon a well-known and well-loved portion of scripture is used to relate man's circumstantial living to his ultimate goals, which include: a clear sense of understanding, a deep sense of reality, and a sustaining quality of faith. This sermon does not work with empty and false promises but demands clear thinking and a mature sense of values. The insecure can be lifted above petty patterns of escape and childish dependency by the obligation to face the meaning of adult adjustment and mature dependency.

III

In a world of rapid change people become confused because the things they have learned to depend on for security are shaken or gone. G. Curtis Jones deals with this situation in a sermon that urges men to look to those things having an element of permanence in their changing nature.

THE SECRET OF PERMANENCE IN A WORLD OF CHANGE [2]

Text: "For it was founded upon a rock."—MATT. 7:25

There are shaking foundations in the modern world. We cannot

[2] Adapted from "The Secret of Permanence in a World of Change," *The Upper Room Pulpit*," April, 1951. Used by permission.

ignore the fact. Our ability to see clearly what is shaking also helps us to judge more accurately what is not being moved. A fine athlete may be destroyed by a weakness for alcohol because he has built on an inadequate foundation. But in contrast is the multitude of godly men who have not been shaken by the circumstances of life simply because they practiced self-discipline.

William Temple said: "God minus the world equals God. The world minus God equals nothing." The stability of any life, or way of life, is not determined by adherence to worldly standards of judgment but rather by an understanding of eternal principles. John Marshall realized that when he built into the Constitution the ethical insights that grew from his own religious awareness. That basic law of the land has stood as a guarantor of human values ever since. It was built on a rock.

The Church has survived through the ages. It has made mistakes and revealed shortcomings. Time has sloughed these off, however, and preserved the essential nature of the Church because, in essence, it attests to a faith in a quality of life determined by eternal spiritual principles rather than man-made and temporal judgments. In that sense the church is a "colony of heaven" where men may find a clarification of values and a purity of motivation. It, too, is built upon the rock.

Jesus points the way. He lived in unstable times, but he found a spiritual relationship to God that gave him guidance, courage, and compassion. He still points the way, as the revelation of the way of life built on unshakeable foundations.

In this sermon the preacher does not deal with insecurities directly; instead he brings the focus of thought to bear on those values that survive the changes tending to breed insecurity. A strong and well-grounded faith stands as the best protection against emotional insecurity.

CHAPTER VI

Preaching to the Lonely

In many respects ours is a lonely age. We have increased the means for communication but we have decreased the capacity for the type of communication that is needed to sustain the souls of men. We can talk across long distances. We can amplify the human voice. We can record the word, write the word, speak the word, even make the word visible; yet we find it difficult to bridge the barriers that exist between one soul and another.

In the face of the equipment for mutuality, we thus find a great amount of frustrating loneliness. Some of this is due to the very complexity of life itself. Three men sit down together. They are all doctors of philosophy. They would be expected to have a common bond of knowledge which would enable them to enjoy a rich experience of intellectual sharing. One is a research chemist, and the long names of compounds with which he is at home are completely unknown to his companions. Another is a sociologist who has spent years making statistical studies of criminals. He knows so much about his subject that he is consulted by authorities in government and education, but there is little about his subject that would make possible a soul-sharing evening with his companions. The third member of the group is a specialist in economics. He knows more about how to predict trends in the market than anyone for miles around, but of course he needs many pages of charts and graphs to show how market trends develop. He cannot carry such equipment about with him, so he is not able to make his best contribution to the discussion. After a sincere and earnest effort to find some area of common interest where they could have a stimulating conversation, the men settle back with their pipes and, in frustrating loneliness of spirit, allow two inane comedians on the TV screen to insult their individual and collective intelligence.

Like hundreds of thousands of other young people, Janet had come to the city to work. She was physically lonely. She just wanted someone close by to touch. Every day she was jostled in the subway crowd, but that was different. Human contact there was careless and without thought or meaning. She wanted someone who cared whether she were near or not. Yes, Janet was sentimental but she had always been in a home where people were not afraid to show affection, and she missed it terribly.

Craig had been in the Army for just a bit more than six months. He had gone through basic training and now was stationed at a base where there was not too much to do. Most of the men found types of amusement that violated his moral standards. He wanted the companionship of the men in his unit but he could not bring himself to do some of the things they did. As a result, he was excluded from much of their activity and often obliged to be by himself. They seemed to respect his standards and, after the first few times, did not bother him. He stayed in his quarters when off duty, studying and writing letters; but he knew he was lonely and sometimes it seemed that he would be willing to compromise some of his standards if he could just be a part of the human activity about him.

Elaine had thyroid trouble. Most of the girls in the freshman class in college were interested in clothes, dates, and sororities. But Elaine weighed over two hundred pounds and was quite self-conscious about it. She did not like to be continually explaining the physical difficulty that was related to her weight, and when she overheard some unkind remarks about it she withdrew from the group. She did not get any invitations to join a sorority, and that hurt too. At home there had been friends who understood and took her for what she was. Here she seemed to be taken for something that she was not. More and more she felt excluded and soon she became bitter. The good-natured girl she had once been now disappeared to make room for a lonely, heartsick girl.

In any congregation there are sure to be the intellectually, physically, morally, or socially lonely. Their loneliness may cause them to withdraw from human relations or to participate at a superficial level. They are apt to be disturbed in interpersonal relations. Often they are persons with rather rigid behavior patterns who find it difficult to adapt or adjust to new circumstances. Often they are introspective and feel that no one cares or really understands their needs and interests. While many people find refreshment and relaxation in being alone, the lonely find their solitude disquieting.

Much of this is probably due to the fact that loneliness starts within the person. A secure person can enjoy being alone with himself, and he can also enjoy the company of others when occasion affords. The lonely person is an inadequate one. He needs emotional support but often does not know how to get it. He needs people and yet he is apt to alienate them. He wants people near and yet is often antagonistic toward them. He wants to accept and reject at the same time. This tendency stems from a basic uncertainty about himself. The lonely person is what might be called a psychic hermit.

A physical hermit finds the life of the community so painful to his nature that he withdraws from it. He rejects society. The psychic hermit lives in society physically but is unable to relate to it psychically. He rejects a portion of social life because it is painful. Yet he longs for some of its satisfactions because life without them is also painful. His feelings may be rooted in antisocial conditions stimulated in early life. He may be responding to circumstantial factors that are more than he can handle, so he withdraws from them. The preacher must be aware of those in his congregation who are in it physically, but out of it emotionally. They may come in late, speak to no one, leave quickly, and perhaps comment to others that it is a cold and unfriendly church.

On the other hand, there are those who are rejected or excluded by society. Here the matter of race, belief, personal characteristics, social status, or group loyalties may be at work. Even within churches a cruel type of exclusiveness is sometimes at work. The pastor is often aware of the injury that is worked by this sense of exclusiveness, and the suffering and loneliness that is its by-product.

The preacher who is aware of the problem of the lonely and the two major conditions that generate it—personality inadequacy and social exclusiveness—may deal helpfully with the situation from the pulpit. He may handle the subject in a full sermonic treatment, or he may use illustrative material that would approach the problem obliquely. He can deal with the question constructively on at least four different levels.

First, he can touch on the loneliness that starts with the mood of withdrawal. Those who deal with mental health problems feel that withdrawal is a symptom of a serious intrapsychic disturbance. In its early stages the situation may be helped or corrected by encouraging the type of involvement with others which will stimulate a group activity that is not too individually threatening. Both schizophrenia and paranoid states show marked withdrawal symptoms. While it is not claimed that preaching can cure the basic emotional states revealed, it is true that healthy

72

group involvement can help the person so afflicted to continue to operate with a larger measure of personal efficiency.

Second, the preacher can deal with the loneliness that stems from uncertainty of self. A group-organized church gives an opportunity for persons to be drawn out, through small group activities that are intimate enough to offer some of the supporting influence of the family without its threatening factors. The preacher can deal frankly with the function and purpose of group involvement as a factor in personality health.

Third, the pastor, in preaching, can so interpret the factors in modern life that stimulate loneliness that those who feel separated may be able to understand their situation more adequately and make the effort that will relate them at a point of common interest. He can deal with the function of the church in bringing people together, despite varied interests and backgrounds, in a common quest for the meaning of life and God's purpose for them. Such a quest can make their routine activities and special interests secondary to an important common experience.

Fourth, the pulpit may deal frankly with those attitudes which cruelly exclude persons from human fellowship on the basis of false and unreasonable judgments. He can interpret the defensive measures that are a part of the practice of exclusion. He can encourage the re-evaluation that is necessary for growth into more adequate judgments of self and others, as well as the meaning of the artificial barriers that men build to protect their false values and prejudices.

As always, in dealing with the problems of preaching, it is important to sense the mind of Christ. Here, that mind is explicit. At no point is Jesus more clear than at the point of the danger of separation from the group. The three parables of separation may well become the bases for three sermons. In the parable of the lost coin, separation is accidental. The coin had no purpose when not in circulation, and all rejoiced when it was again being useful as its nature intended. The lost sheep, with its nose to the ground, became separated through carelessness. But the sheep was not safe when separated, and great effort was exerted to make him a part of the flock again. The lost son was separated by willful design. He was a great concern to his father and to himself until he was again restored to a right relationship to his family. In each instance Jesus points out that separation is a real danger and that re-establishing right relations is the solution.

Preaching to the needs of the lonely suggests at least the three following emphases.

I

The first sermon seeks to interpret the importance of group relationship for each individual. By interpreting our nature and the way the group acts in relation to that nature, this sermon indicates the important contribution of the group to life.

THE SOCIAL FUNCTION OF RELIGION

Text: *"For where two or three are gathered together in my name, there am I in the midst of them."*—MATT. 18:20

The importance of group involvement. Human beings are social creatures. They are born into a group, the family. They are educated in groups called classes. They worship in groups called parishes. Much of life is a group experience. We are beings who need group support. Even the small group serves its purpose by giving a chance for expression and experimental growth in thinking and feeling. The so-called "herd instinct" seems to be a fact of experience even though it may not be established as a premise in social science. We cannot live the life of a human being apart from the social group.

The importance of group purpose. The equality of the group

does much to determine the character and usefulness of its members. Some groups create and others destroy. The group relationships that best sustain life's great purposes are those that take God into account. It is even more significant if God is made the central, all-important fact by which group activity is determined.

The nature of group fulfillment. Group involvement that is purposive and oriented about a quest for God's will, not only gives to life a valid emotional support and a sense of moral values, but it meets the needs of man's social nature at the highest possible level, opening the way for the achievement of true spiritual grandeur. Worship involves a group, and true worship invites the ultimate in group or social fulfillment in common devotion and inspiration before God.

Through this type of sermon those who have allowed themselves to become withdrawn may be stimulated to take a more active interest in group life and those who have an active group life may be stimulated to reach out to persons seemingly unrelated in order that their need for group life may be met.

II

Where separation from the group may be the result of factors beyond the control of the individual—racial, social, or economic exclusion, or even the price paid for moral courage—the lonely may find support in cosmic companionship.

THE MEANING OF COSMIC FRIENDSHIP

Text: *"And underneath are the everlasting arms."*—DEUT. 33:27

Life acquires an added sense of security when it feels that the essential quality of the universe is friendly, rather than antagonistic, toward the quest for life's meaning. There are times when self-confidence is shaken. There are other times when our confidence in mankind is weakened. If at such times we can see in the universe

75

the even movement of divine purpose and the sustaining order of God's law, our living is made more certain.

When it seems that life is exacting the price that must be paid for moral courage, there is deep satisfaction in feeling that in God's wise economy there is that orderliness that preserves the good and will not allow its ultimate destruction. There is strength to undergird life in the faith that the very structure of the universe, from the stars in their courses to the electrons in theirs, is dedicated to a purpose worthy of our devotion.

The great naturalists—Thoreau, Burroughs, Burbank, Carver— though they varied in the degree of their orthodoxy, did not vary in their humility before the orderliness of a nature that revealed a Mind both creative and friendly. To be at home in the universe, to accept the essentially friendly nature of our cosmic home, is to give to life a quality that brings both long-range perspective and present emotional support.

Another dimension is added to prayer, both personal and corporate, when we feel deeply that "the eternal God is thy refuge, and underneath are the everlasting arms."

The dependable, orderly nature of the universe can give strength to those who feel withdrawn from other friendly relations; for the universe is the primal home and within its order and moral law the courageous can find companionship. The prophet is often a lover of flowers and the world of nature. This sermon is designed to stimulate just such a feeling within the mind and heart of the listener.

III

The individuality of religion often causes a feeling of aloneness. As the relationship with God is intensely personal, it must always be cultivated in the inner recesses of one's own soul. In this sermon Boynton Merrill indicates the important positive factors that are related to this feeling of loneliness.

ON BEING ALONE [1]

Text: *"He was there alone."*—MATT. 14:23

If we are intent on certain goals we must often travel alone. Because other people may travel toward lesser goals does not become the final determinant of our values.

Real religion is a deep inner response to life. As such it must be intensely personal. It must grow out of creative use of solitariness.

To be lonely and to be alone are quite different. We can be lonely when we are not alone, and we can be alone with no sense of loneliness.

Jesus often went alone to pray in order to gain strength and give direction to his life. For him it was a way of restoring right relations with God so that he might keep a right attitude toward himself and those about him.

The mystics knew how to find the values of solitude. The great figures of religious history were often alone in meditation. For some it was the aloneness of exile, as John on Patmos. Again, it was the aloneness of jail, as with Bunyan and Fox. For others it was aloneness by choice, as St. Francis and Gandhi.

Even the lonely soul is not entirely alone. Paganini was able to make music with one string alone. God can still use you as an instrument when you are alone—with him.

It is important for one to learn the values that can be created in solitude. Sometimes periods of enforced loneliness become real opportunities for spiritual growth. This sermon indicates the possibility and stimulates the use of it.

[1] Adapted from "On Being Alone" in *Arrows of Light* (New York: Harper & Bros., 1935). Used by permission.

CHAPTER VII

Preaching to the Defeated

For many, life is a battle. Overborne by the struggle and over-burdened by a feeling that they cannot cope with opposing forces, they live conscious of the strain of competition and apprehensive of defeat. While some competition may be stimulating, certain types of personality do not function well under the persistent pressure of competitive action. Some reach a breaking point and fall by the wayside. Others transmit their defeat to those over whom they have dominance. Still others adjust to a lower level of accomplishment because they are afraid of the injuries that may come through competition.

Our society gives a high place to competitive action. Competition early becomes a part of the school experience. Numerical grades become a standard of judgment of performance. Sports activity is determined by the ability to win. Community life may be permeated by a struggle for status, "to keep up with the Joneses." Many persons who do not have a large measure of aggressiveness in their natures find it difficult to operate in such a system.

Strenuous competition inevitably causes casualties. Some children, early aware of their inability to compete effectively in school, become problems to themselves and others by projecting their attitude of defeat into overtly destructive behavior. They

are continuing to compete but at a different level and with dis-
approved methods. Their misdirected competitive activity may
bring them into open conflict with the community, and before
they find out the nature of their feelings they may have been
permanently injured.

The projection of the mood of competition into family life has
injurious effects. It is probably most graphically seen in suburbia,
where efforts are made to attain a social status through competitive social activity. The result is often injurious to the persons
involved, for social life then becomes a means to an end rather
than an end in itself. Social relationships then tend to disrupt
rather than sustain life. The real blessings of sustaining friendship are lost in a quest for lesser values. Often, established standards which tend to stabilize life are sacrificed to the pressure of
competition, and large numbers of these persons injured by competition become problem drinkers and trouble-making neurotics.
Their condition marks a further injurious effect of competition.

Often, without realizing what is at the bottom of their inner
turmoil, persons are carrying on within themselves a civil war
between the values of a ruthlessly competitive society and the
standards of Christian idealism. Such conflict may be guilt-creat-
ing as well as disrupting of personal efficiency. Sometimes it is resolved by accepting the moral standards of the world of business
and carrying on the ethical standards of Christianity in only a
verbal and detached way. At other times, the judgments of religion become so important that the whole approach to business
life is re-examined and re-evaluated.

Whichever way the person moves in resolving the inner conflict that is set up by such choices of values, it seems inevitable
that a measure of defeat is sustained by him. However he may
rationalize the process, he cannot but feel the corrosive effect
upon life when he sees the values by which he has lived being

persistently defeated by the pressures of business and social life. On the other hand, there are those whose rigid adherence to ethical standards demands of them a price in terms of acceptance and success that they are not willing to pay; and though they adhere, they do it with resentment and self-pity that is equally disruptive of emotional health and happiness.

What have we to say to persons who are emmeshed in this type of defeat? What can we do to relieve the sense of depression that may envelop life as the result of such inner conflict or external disappointment? What has our Christian message to say in a day when the conflict between material and spiritual standards of life is often made explicit in the life and confusion and defeat of those who are caught in the struggle?

It is important to sense the dynamic factors at work in the personalities of such competition-weary and defeated persons. One reaction may be that of withdrawal from sustaining social relations. The world of conflict may be so emotionally disturbing that a preoccupation with hobbies, or research, or intellectual escape may increasingly occupy the person. While such things in and of themselves may be useful for relaxation, they create a problem when they become a substitute for an important area of life activity. They become dangerous when they shut out family and other sustaining group activities.

The more usual response to this conflict is probably an atrophy of values and a sense of depression. How often in the counseling room a man will list the nature of the problems that stem from an atrophying of values and then say cynically, "Is life worth the trouble?" How could the self-destructive nature of a loss of values be demonstrated more graphically?

Defeat and depression seem to walk hand in hand, but the nature of the depression can show itself in at least three ways. The first would be an aggressive attitude toward one's self. The individual blames himself for failures and assesses his worth negatively to others. He condemns himself often and without reason and becomes fearful of taking initiative, for he sees failure as the inevitable outcome of whatever he tries.

Some persons live in a mild state of depression for long periods of time, remaining sensitive, quick tempered, and hard to live with. They willingly adopt habits and types of behavior that are mildly self-destructive. While they may not consciously recognize the fact, their attitude toward themselves and the value of life itself may make them more prone to self-injuring accidents. Their attitude in social relations may be careless and self-damaging just as their behavior in the family framework may rob them of the real possibilities of love and happiness. When such pressures are placed upon life that persons can no longer adjust, it is not a far move from the unconscious self-destructive behavior of the mildly depressed person to the suicidal threat of the severely depressed individual.

Some who are depressed will express it in aggressiveness toward others. They are the type who may feel that they must give ulcers as a self-defense against getting them. Cynical, sullen, distrustful, and unsympathetic, they operate far below their level of potential because they are involved in working out their aggressions destructively rather than creatively. Though they are defeated individuals, they are unable to free themselves from the mood of the battle to rise to a higher plane of orientation. Unable to win against those who represent the real competition of life, they persist in making victims of those who would normally win their protection and sympathetic understanding. Tyrants at home, troublemakers in the community, and creators of dissension and discord in the church, they are projecting their inner defeat into the outer relationships of life with a vengeance.

The third type of reaction to depression might be called a

81

rejection of the universe. Of course this would vary in degree and never be complete, for life could not be sustained by a negativism that touched all of its areas. Mr. B. might illustrate this type. He had been a successful businessman, an official of the church, and a local leader. Severe financial reverses impaired his business and sent him into a state of depression. He resigned from the church, saying, "If God does that sort of thing to me I want no part of him." He withdrew from community leadership. In effect, he tried to project his defeat back into the very structure of the universe. For him, it was no longer governed by law and order, but by whim. Rather than accept his defeat as a part of a competitive struggle he blamed it on the unpredictable quality of the universe. Hard, bitter, withdrawn, he drew the battle lines between himself and the universe at large and, for the rest of his life, suffered from the quality of inevitable defeat that comes from such irrational projection of inner feelings into outer circumstance.

Persons who have suffered personality injury through weariness or defeat in the competitive struggles of life may well find that they need to keep a sense of values and a sense of perspective by means of the mental stimulation and spiritual inspiration that may come through well directed pulpit utterance.

A major problem of our day is the atrophy of love. Psychoanalysts say they merely try to remove the blocks to a healthy capacity to express love. The basic demand of our religion is to love neighbor as self. Much of the conflict that is life-defeating is an outgrowth of the demand that human considerations be made secondary to the demands of material success. When the order can be reversed, much of the satisfaction of life can be reclaimed. Surely there is no task that is better suited to the traditions and nature of the preaching ministry.

Sermons can be instruments for turning defeat into victory

by helping to change the standards of judgment for success. When a man comes to church depressed in spirit because his actions have denied the tenets of his faith, he needs to be inspired with a courage to see himself as he is, to re-examine the basis of his behavior, and to take the action that will bring it into accord with his faith. Only then will he find peace within. If, in his inner struggle for values, he cannot find help from the church, he has suffered a grievous denial. Week in and week out, the church can stand for those values that will sustain the best in life. The sermon, as an instrument of insight, can make explicit the values that each individual can examine and use in the context of his life. Then the man who has felt defeat may begin to evaluate himself more fairly and, from depression, may grow toward new hope and new effort.

Sermons can be instruments for turning defeat into victory by helping people to learn how to adjust to failure. Each person must sustain some failure. The ability to grow through failure enriches the experience of those who endure it. A publisher of popular books recently asked an author to write a simple book on those persons who have made victorious lives out of defeating circumstances. The thesis is that the quality of victory is developed from within rather than acquired from without, and that if persons can learn this capacity for inner adequacy they will turn even the most disturbing circumstances to good ends. This theme might well fit in with the belief that God's end for man is a spiritual victory that makes even crosses the symbols of eternal life, and chains, the mark of an ambassador.

Failure itself may be a way toward life. Sometimes material failures release the power of the soul for new and wonderful discoveries about life. As failure may begin within the spirit of the individual, so also spiritual adequacy must be a product of the life that has gained mastery over self, to the extent that it can control the self in situations that might be defeat-creating. Failure is often not so much a fact as it is an attitude. Those who concentrate on their inadequacies are apt to project them. Those who develop their spiritual resources are surely going to have opportunities to use them. The sermon may well consider the attitude toward failure and the type of orientation that can move beyond such failures so that they become incidents in a larger process rather than dead-end streets for living.

One never knows the state of mind of those who sit before him. But it is well within the bounds of reason to believe that in our day many who come to worship are disturbed by inner conflicts, burdened by a sense of defeat, and threatened by states of depression that can impair their efficiency as persons, though they may not lead to complete destruction. Such persons have a right to expect a sense of hope, an utterance of faith, and a quality of inspiration that can help their flagging spirits.

The following sermon résumés indicate how this has been done by others who have faced the problem and have tried to give a realistic answer in sermonic form.

I

John Sutherland Bonnell, who early and effectively employed modern psychological insight in preaching, has a message for the defeated and depressed that starts with an acceptance of the feelings of those in a gray mood, but moves beyond it with constructive suggestion and confident insight to turn gray days into times of spiritual opportunity.

COURAGE FOR THE DISCOURAGED [1]

Text: *"For our high priest is not one who is incapable of sympathy with our weaknesses, but he has been tempted in*

[1] Adapted from "Courage for the Discouraged" in *What Are You Living For?* (New York and Nashville: Abingdon Press, 1950). Used by permission.

*every way just as we have, without committing any sin.
So let us come with courage to God's throne of grace to
receive his forgiveness and find him responsive when we
need his help."*—HEB. 4:15-16 (Goodspeed)

Religion divorced from life becomes a cold, dead formalism. It
holds no hope, for it deals with no real needs.

Religion is helpful when it practices no elements not also available to us. Jesus met the temptations of life and proved adequate
because he believed in a dependable cause-effect relationship at work.
Standing as we stand, he fought the battles of life. He promised no
easy victories, but he revealed a never-failing courage based on ultimate faith in God's goodness.

In crises Jesus prayed, for in prayer his courage was confirmed.
When men were cruel, he tried to see something in them which
was above cruelty and to appeal to that quality. He had courage to
look for the best in other people.

In the case of the woman taken in adultery, the Pharisees were
concerned about her condemnation, while Jesus was concerned about
her salvation. A great purpose clarifies motivation and strengthens
courage to look beyond the incidents that disturb to the possibilities
that exist.

With the example of Jesus before us, there is no reason why we
should ever give in to defeat. He speaks from the heat of the moral
battle. He indicates a moral power that can give meaning to real
courage. When he looks at us with our failures, he is not interested
in condemning, but in helping us to move beyond discouragement
and failure to effective action and abundant living.

When life becomes difficult, keep your eye on the great Captain
of your salvation. He will help you to believe in yourself. He will
call out the splendid within you. There is true courage when it is
needed most.

A sermon of this type gives perspective. It comes to grips emotionally and intellectually with the problem of depressed spirits.

Gray is the color of depression. The gray look, the gray feeling, the gray attitude—they are the result of confused values. When we no longer have the moral courage to see the distinction between black and white, all of life suffers. By emphasizing the importance of perspective, moral courage, and staying power, the defeated and depressed person is met where he is and moved to a higher level of adequacy. In religious faith he finds new hope, new faith in himself, and new faith in the long process that is sometimes needed to achieve worthy goals. Because he comes to believe in himself again, he can believe in life and is then able to live it with more courage.

II

Speaking directly to the matter of values sufficient to sustain life, Halford E. Luccock preached a sermon that uses frames of reference close at hand to the average listener in order to illuminate a text from Deuteronomy.

ON TRIAL FOR YOUR LIFE [2]

Text: *"Thy life shall hang in doubt before thee."*—Deut. 28:66

Using the comment of a playwright that the New York telephone directory doesn't have much of a plot but a tremendous cast, he indicates that for many the experience of life is all cast and no plot. Unless there can be some great purpose to tie the experiences of life together, it falls into a variety of meaningless events. We are continually on trial to establish a sense of values large enough to make life more than assorted experiences, good or bad.

We are on trial for the life of our minds. Are they merely to accept the avalanche of assorted facts and opinions that pour into them; or are we to develop an inner capacity to evaluate, accept, and reject. Unless we develop that capacity, our minds can become a

[2] Adapted from "On Trial for Your Life" in *Marching off the Map* (New York: Harper & Bros., 1952). Used by permission.

menace rather than a divine instrument, especially in a day of the "big lie."

Also we are on trial for our souls. Empty ideas of success do not nourish the spirits of men. We keep our values keen by nourishing our souls so that they remain alive and vigorous. A soul can never become a frozen asset. A close walk with Jesus keeps the soul alive and values clearly defined.

In this sermon Luccock dramatizes the role that values play in bringing our lives together in a purposeful experience. The sermon challenges its hearers to fight against the forces that would atrophy values and to work diligently for a view of life that makes the best not only desirable but essential.

III

In the following sermon the preacher deals with the fact that sooner or later we all realize that we are persons with liabilities as well as assets. Our lives depend upon the capacity we develop for handling our liabilities creatively.

MAKING ASSETS OF YOUR LIABILITIES

Text: "For my strength is made perfect in weakness."—II COR. 12:9

Often a crippling circumstance becomes an "Open sesame." One need only mention the familiar names of Michelangelo, Milton, Beethoven, Darwin, Stevenson, and Helen Keller to know what we mean by making assets of liabilities.

The unseen liabilities are often those of circumstance and emotional injury, but they too may be made into assets. The bereaved may become more sympathetic, the defeated may become more understanding, the soul buffeted by circumstance may develop new capacities in compensation. To develop his voice, Roland Hayes struggled against poverty and racial discrimination. His mother, a former slave, was his best coach for he had to enunciate clearly to make her understand. Thus he developed perfect diction.

87

The attitude of mind becomes the active ingredient in determining whether any given circumstance becomes an asset or a liability. Rembrandt used shadows to create new depth in painting. The shadows of life may deepen insight and value.

Jesus was rejected, betrayed, deserted, condemned, and executed; yet he has taught more about life than any other person who ever lived. Through a great faith he turned every unfortunate circumstance into a steppingstone. He did not measure circumstances by man's judgment but sought instead to make them a revelation of God's larger purpose.

When life and its limitations are accepted without self-pity but with faith, we are prepared to make the greatest possible use of each day. A sustaining faith then keeps us from bowing before weakness, liability, or trouble, and helps us to keep the momentum of motion toward positive goals. "Cowards die many times before their deaths; the valiant never taste of death but once." Even then, through our faith, death becomes but another circumstance that the valiant spirit surmounts.

This sermon helps each person to fit his particular liability or problem into a larger context. Moving beyond depression and self-pity, he is able to see new resources for life in an active faith, and new privileges in each day as he seeks to do God's will rather than his own.

CHAPTER VIII

Preaching to the Angry

One does not work with people long before realizing that there are some persons who approach every life situation defensively. Sometimes this defensive quality is shown by barriers, and at other times by the psychological equivalent of the military axiom that the best defense is a strong offense. Such persons live with a "chip on their shoulder." They are quick to combat and seem to be continually in a state of anger against some person or some cause. That there are a large number of such people in our society is attested by the fact that certain magazines and newspapers which give journalistic expression to this mood of persistent anger are well supported. These are the persons who are always itching for a fight, and the cause itself is secondary to their inner need to be giving expression to a build-up of angry feelings.

Such a state of mind is not necessarily willful or conscious. As the philosopher Immanuel Kant long ago observed, "The cry of a child newly borne has the tone not of lamentation but of wrath." The birth experience in and of itself may be so organically painful that the growing personality has a backlog of anger against life. If this is so there may be a backlog of anger within the personality that breaks out in a variety of human relations. To overcome such an unconscious mood of anger, a person must learn a new way of facing life and its experience; or as Jesus put it, he must go through the experience of birth again with a more mature capacity for evaluating its effects. From the view of a modern psychologist the feeling of the child about life is real and honest and cannot be adequately dealt with apart from reality and honesty. The child reacts vigorously against pain and any situation that is pain-creating. This innate anger must be conditioned by a process of evaluating experience until a person arrives at the state where he chooses some painful experiences because he sees in them greater values. Birth may be painful but to be deprived of parenthood would be even more so. The personality is continually being born into a new sense of relationship to its innate anger. But as the process is a continuing one, so also the assistance in coping with it must continue.

Many of the experiences of childhood are anger-producing but are met on such a basis that the anger cannot be expressed. We are told that the child's delight in stories about giants is closely related to his desire to see little people overcome their big and blundering enemies. Certainly adults must appear formidable to the small child, and the power of the adult to manipulate and control the activity of the child must often create anger that may be suppressed, forced back into the unconscious, and at a later time becomes a factor in adult behavior. A child who often watched a drunken father abuse her mother has shown results of the anger in an adult disdain of all men, and although comely has refused to marry. Her displaced anger is still being expressed indirectly against men in general, to the end that she is denying herself the privileges and responsibilities of normal, adult family life. The only hope of deliverance for her is to be born again into a new and healthier relationship to her own emotions and her group feelings.

It is unfortunate indeed when the anger one feels is so displaced that it is worked out against the self. Such displaced anger may be called masochism or a martyr complex. Of course, there is a sharp distinction between those who are willing to stand for a matter of principle in spite of consequence and those who persistently invite self-injury as an end in itself emotionally. In severe cases, specialized therapy is needed to release the normal healthy emotions. But for many of those persons who suffer from a fringe or marginal difficulty with anger feelings, the sermon that helps them to see the cause-effect relationship of their behavior can be useful indeed. It can help the individual to understand his anger as a mechanism of defense against deep-rooted antagonisms. He may be led to see the inadequacy of such irrational attitudes and such throwbacks to immature methods of dealing with life experience. He may be led to see the relation between the tantrum mood and the use of force in human relations, sensing it as an admission of an inability to adjust reasonably to the problems that life presents.

Usually the person dominated by anger is not happy about the condition. He knows that it continually causes him difficulty. He does not want to make enemies or lose his capacity to operate effectively. In boxing, the advantage immediately goes to the one who can make his opponent angry, for anger makes him careless. A baseball pitcher once remarked that he often became angry but found that he had to learn to master his anger to keep from "blowing" the game. When he was dominated by anger he lost the fine edge on his control. Often the person with angry responses is aware of the difficulty and is seeking some basis for handling it. It may be that the sermon will provide the way of self-understanding that can bring self-mastery.

But often anger is cleverly disguised. Civilization places a severe restraint on the expression of our aggressive feelings. The structure of civilized relationships is built on rationalized anger and sublimated aggressiveness. Often without understanding the mechanism at work, a person will drive himself into vigorous work or sublimate his anger in socially acceptable behavior. This may be all that he needs to keep his angry feelings under control. Others may need to be continually reminded of the importance of keeping their feelings in check so that they may live more happily within themselves and in relation to other people.

Karen Horney has given a helpful interpretation of the way in which the personality comes to deal with the inner conflicts that affect human behavior. She speaks of those who react against others in aggressive behavior, those who reach away from other people in withdrawal, and those who move toward other people in dependence and reconciliation. Such a basic insight into the behavior of persons could well become the basis for some helpful pulpit interpretation. Each of the types of behavior could be illustrated from the Scriptures. Saul, the king, was the great "anti-person" of the Old Testament. He was a fighter against all his neighbors and their gods, but he never had anything positive at the core of his own life, and his mind was finally destroyed by his unrestrained anger. As the inner conflicts of Judas increased he sought escape through withdrawal. First, he withdrew from a sense of group responsibility, then from the disciples, and further from the Jewish community to which he had a questionable loyalty, until that final act of withdrawal enacted in self-destruction. The movement away from people tends to be a partial and psychic form of suicide for human beings, who are essentially social beings with a way of life that is sustained by group relationships. In the woman at the well in Samaria, Jesus recognized a person who moved toward other people but only to find frustration and failure. Consort of many men, she had lost her status in the community and was living as an outcast. Her quest for love had been immature, irresponsible, and frustrating. Jesus helped her to find herself and a spiritual principle large enough to bring insight, honesty, and a genuine concern for others.

Since anger is an active denial of the principle of love, it becomes a destructive force directed against the self in derision, against others in active resentments, and against God in cynicism and hypocrisy. The original purpose of anger at the animal level is no longer served in the life of modern society. The animal mechanism for shooting adrenalin into the blood and stimulating the fighting instinct is still a part of us but is clearly atavistic. As we have brought other primitive instinctive drives under control, so we must develop the resources of mind and society to handle this life-disrupting force.

The Scriptures equate the angry person with the fool. We realize, usually too late, that the angry approach to any human situation is unproductive. We usually make fools of ourselves in a quite literal sense when we are angry, but we often place ourselves in a mood to learn about ourselves and our relations to others as we look carefully at our foolish behavior. To assist us we have certain scriptural admonitions that may well be the basis for sermonic consideration.

First, there is the invitation to rational evaluation. Let your answers be simple expressions of "yes" or "no" rather than an appeal to emotion or religious authority. When an answer is a simple expression of personal conviction it is less inflammatory and more convincing than when it carries the burden of personal offensiveness but does not give a clear expression of opinion.

Second, there is the admonition to constructive activity. When one gets busy about something worth doing there is less inclination to say things that are not worth saying. No word of the Good Samaritan is recorded; yet his action that bridged the barriers of race, nationality, and creed continues to be a challenge to the petty angers that complicate life and separate people.

Third, there is the need to learn to endure deprivation. Not all situations in life will develop to suit our immediate and selfish desires. We learn to adjust to realities and such an adjustment diminishes our personal sensitivity and widens our perspective. To be able to say in a variety of life situations, "Not my will, but thine," is to be able to adjust to a purpose larger than immature sensitivity. It is an indication of the ability to operate beyond the small anger-producing motives. When we learn to give up small, selfish purposes for larger, unselfish purposes, we have effectively separated ourselves from most of the situations that would touch off the angry response.

Each of these three areas of consideration is well within the range of the traditional sermon. Yet each could speak directly to the person who is struggling against a mood and attitude that is complicating life for him and for others. Perhaps the following sermon résumés will indicate in greater detail how this might be done.

I

The psychotherapist speaks of a syndrome as a group of symptoms that supplement each other in revealing a certain type of morbid emotional state. Paul, in writing to the Ephesians, gathers together in one sentence the characteristics of the angry person and invites his reader to put aside such attitudes. Paul knows how disruptive such feelings are in the life of the church and the individuals in it. He knows because there was a time when he lived with and was driven by these same emotions.

94

HOW TO OVERCOME ANGER

Text: *"Let all bitterness, and wrath, and anger, and clamour, and evil speaking, be put away from you, with all malice."*—Eph. 4:31

Paul pictures the mounting destructiveness of angry feelings. Growing out of bitterness, seething in wrath and welling up in anger, and finally bursting forth with the uncontrolled noisiness of the clamorous person in words that injure and cripple personalities —this, says Paul, is the way anger works.

We have seen it. It starts from small inner hurts and explodes in far-reaching and disruptive action. Probably all of us have watched a person smolder in bitterness and explode in anger with all of the words and actions that go with such anger. We have also seen the wreckage that such anger leaves in the lives of persons, homes, organizations, and communities—even among nations. Such phrases as "Remember the Alamo," "Remember the Maine," and "Remember Pearl Harbor," are used, not so much to bring clear understanding of international relations and a clear approach to justice, as to stimulate bitterness and excite the type of anger that sends men off to fight.

But Paul was not satisfied to describe a process. He prescribed an antidote. Let such emotions "be put away from you, with all malice." He indicates that we begin to deal with the emotional expressions when we deal with the source. Abraham Lincoln realized the same thing when he said, "With malice toward none, and charity for all."

The syndrome of unbalanced emotions growing out of anger can be noted in the breakup of the home, in international relations, in racial relations, and in the varied aspects of interpersonal relations. Irrational factors destroy perspective. But the way to health and peaceful living can be found when we move toward good will and understanding and a view of life without malice.

Through being possessed by the mind of Christ, Paul found a way beyond malice. Every life can have a Damascus Road experience when a great new light breaks through to dispel the bitterness that destroys, using the more mature judgment that redeems and releases.

Such a sermon puts into religious context the type of emotional growth that is needed to live above the anger-producing emotions that can waylay life. But this ability to live above such feelings is not accidental. It comes through a new set of emotional responses dictated by a new mind, a new way of looking at life and human experience.

II

This sermon is a variation on the last one but does not deal with the matter so much in terms of a great transformation as it does a slow process of mastery.

LEARNING TO CONTROL YOUR TEMPER

Text: *"Let every man be swift to hear, slow to speak, slow to wrath: for the wrath of man worketh not the righteousness of God."*—JAS. 1:19-20

How easily we ascribe to our angry impulses the dignity of righteous indignation. How easily we reverse the process of understanding, by refusing to listen to all sides of a question and by speaking quickly and wrathfully.

The apostle James, in his early Christian sermon, invites his listeners to consider several dangerous attitudes and practices. There is the haste that maketh waste because it operates from prejudice and angry feelings rather than information and good will.

There is the danger that develops with angry judgments which are not sound judgments and which make a mockery of the nature of justice itself.

There is the danger that comes from the words of anger—words that injure and distort and destroy.

There is the danger that comes from the reactions that anger starts—violence, injury of others, injury of self, and destruction of values.

These dangers can be brought under control by reversing the

usual processes of anger. Be swift to hear, and listen wisely and well. Be slow to speak and slow to let the wrathful judgment take control. Be wise to label one's own feelings for what they are rather than confuse hateful emotions with righteous indignation. Then self-understanding and understanding of others can open the way for growth and wise action.

Such a sermon, with the use of the kind of practical illustrations that come quickly to mind, can be of immediate help to those who may be involved in anger attitudes that disturb home or life. It can encourage a program of reversed action, which will gradually help to bring unbridled emotions under control.

III

Many life situations can be eased by a sense of humor. While it is not one of the great or traditional Christian virtues, it does have a place in life.

THE SAVING GRACE OF A SENSE OF HUMOR
Text: *"A soft answer turneth away wrath: but grievous words stir up anger."*—PROV. 15:1

Laughter in scriptural context is usually related to derision. But the ability to sense an element of humor in human relations may go far to keep a person from taking himself too seriously. Anger unites a crowd destructively, and we have the lynch mob. Humor can individualize the persons in a crowd and take the sharp edge from its destructiveness. Lincoln used such a technique with a lynch mob and changed not only its mood but its purpose.

A sense of humor is one of the secondary virtues. Sincerity is important but in a secondary sense. To be sincere is not enough, for one may be just as mistaken though he is sincerely mistaken. A sense of humor is not in itself creative, but as the molecules of oil make possible the smooth running of an engine, so also the bits of humor tend to keep life running more smoothly.

97

Humor may be both a conscious and an unconscious defense against the force of anger. In either case it may well serve to keep the person from becoming bogged down in the destructive elements of anger. Even if a sense of humor be nothing but a device, it serves to ease the pressures of life and help to get things done.

The soft answer, the word or phrase that is a friendly gesture, the bit of humor that hurts no one—these release some of the pent-up feelings that otherwise might be expressed in anger and also help the creative process of life to flow more smoothly.

A sermon that deals with a sense of humor will not be profound but it may be genuinely helpful by keeping life in a proper perspective and aiding the smooth progress toward its important goals.

CHAPTER IX

Preaching to Those Who Doubt

Doubt is often a disorganizing factor in life. Many persons in our day are feeling the effects of this doubt. A scientific materialism has undermined many of the traditional beliefs that have made people of past generations feel secure. Where motivation once seemed clear and simple, it is now obscure and complicated. The relations of groups and nations are made difficult by many factors that did not exist a few decades ago. All of these elements of modern life tend to create doubt, and many sensitive souls suffer from a state of perpetual doubt and perplexity.

Often when doubts are expressed in religious terms they but cover other and deeper doubts that affect life. When a person comes to his pastor and indicates that he has doubts about the personal nature of God, he may be saying indirectly that he has severe doubts about the quality of his own personality and its relationship with the structure of the universe. In recent years it has been easier for persons to form a concept of God which is intellectually acceptable than to establish an emotionally satisfying feeling of relationship toward a divine nature. In order to deal with the needs of such persons, we must be concerned, not primarily about the concepts of theology, but rather with establishing healthy attitudes toward the self and toward others and with cosmic reality.

Many persons with doubts do not realize that they are using the fact of doubt pragmatically, just as many other persons establish the value of faith, because it produces desired positive results. Doubts can be cultivated with an unconscious purpose demanded by the personality. Some persons in a state of depression build a structure of doubts that for them becomes the equivalent of suicide. In this form of psychic suicide they project their feelings about themselves and their life into a pattern of intellectual rationalization.

Doubt may be an expression of emotional fatigue. When the demands of a variety of responsibilities press in upon life, a person may be so overcome by fatigue that he begins to doubt his ability to measure up. He may raise questions as to the value of accepting responsibility and then move on to the position that responsibility is to be avoided. The escape from responsibility is often an expression of doubt in action.

Doubt may also be an indication of an escape from reality. When the demands for adjustment to a stern reality are too great, the personality may protect itself from the adjustment by doubting its necessity. This sort of situation is often noted with those who need psychiatric help, for they show their resistance to a real need by developing doubts as to the value, effectiveness, or integrity of psychotherapists. Similarly, those who need the sustaining power of a religious faith but are unwilling to make the personal commitment that is involved, raise all manner of doubts that seem to satisfy, in part at least, their desire to escape from the reality, even though the rationalizations are themselves unreal.

This definition of doubt as a form of neurotic manifestation will raise a question as to the nature of what we call honest doubt. It is important to realize that objective doubt is often an essential part of mature thinking. Growth from immature concepts of

215 58

religion to the more mature judgments of the adults is often accompanied by a type of doubt that is a healthy manifestation. Jesus himself was a constructive doubter. From the time, as a lad, he questioned the elders in the temple until the end of his life, he continually challenged the ideas of the past and the attitudes of the present that were denials of the basic values of human personality.

In approaching his people the pastor must be aware of the two types of doubt and the need for dealing with both constructively. The one is real and must be handled with a concern for the reality factors involved. The other is related to what William James refers to as a disease of the personality, a tendency toward chronic doubt. Honest doubt can usually be handled adequately by a direct approach to the problem involved. If the doubt is honest it will usually be resolved by the direct approach. It is the persistently unresolved, the chronic doubt, that destroys rather than builds and that reveals personality flaws rather than a process of growth.

Because the neurotic form of doubt is often disguised, care must be used in approaching it. The specific problem is but an invitation to explore the "why" that lies behind it. The neurotic doubter's problem is not so much his doubt as it is himself. Doubt concerning the anthropomorphic concept of God may be related to deep feelings of the person about his own father. Doubts about marriage may be related to fears that have been generated by long contact with human relations that were disruptive in the family situation. The early conditioning of the child's life may be an important factor lying behind the doubts that are a verbal form of an expression of concern about life and human relations. If such doubt is carried to its logical conclusion it may well mean a disrupted or destroyed life. If it is met intelligently and with a discernment of the emotional forces at work behind it, it may be the way of freeing life from its crippling fears and releasing the personality for more normal growth toward desired goals and a creative faith.

As a frustrating experience is often a preface to progress, so a doubt may be a prelude to mental and spiritual growth. Because the growth factor is essentially related to developmental forces from within the individual, it is evident that mere authoritarianism may increase frustration and stimulate further doubt. A sermon able to meet both types of doubt creatively must be an affirmation that invites shared mental and emotional participation, rather than a declaration of rigid and unalterable dogma. The process of growth is often stimulated by the head-on collision between an active mind and dogma. Mere dogmatics, then, increase the doubt or move it to a different level of acceptance where temporary adjustment may be made but further doubt, merely postponed.

If faith is to be developed it is important to remember that it develops at three levels. Belief is the intellectual basis for faith. Conviction is the expression of faith at the emotional level. Action is the involvement of the being in the fulfillment of the mental and emotional aspects of faith at the level of the total personality. To establish a level of belief through authoritarian utterance, without building genuine conviction, only increases the chance of deep-seated doubt. The effort to combine belief and conviction with a fear of action will soon kill the sustaining power of any faith. In preaching to overcome doubt, the three levels of faith must be kept always in focus, for to fail to engage the elements of faith at all of the three levels of human experience is to invite the very situation that stimulates doubt.

Thus, preaching to those who doubt requires more than a strong element of affirmation. There must be the element of inspiration that can help to create conviction, as well as specific suggestions for implementing the affirmations in practical action. When one deals with doubts from the pulpit, he must be aware of the fact that there are those with honest doubt as well as those with neurotic doubts before him. A single level of approach to faith may give the neurotic doubter just the excuse he needs for shifting his problem to another level of human experience rather than facing it. If the doubt is essentially a matter of the emotions, he may shift it to the intellectual level and rationalize it. If it is a matter of belief he may transfer it to the level of action and there find the excuse that would further re-inforce his doubt. Also, the honest doubter will see the inadequacy of any approach to faith that neglects one or another of the essential elements of a total faith.

As doubt of self grows from life experience that breeds loss of self-regard, and as doubt of others is the product of antisocial fears, so religious doubts may involve a disorganization of the sense of support for life that healthy purpose brings. Whether it be personal, social, or religious doubt, the important question that must be answered in the mind of the doubter is "Why?" Why does he doubt? What is the basis for the emotional, intellectual, or action problem that is expressed in his doubts?

In conversation and in counseling, the questions may be answered directly or obliquely. In the relation between the pulpit and the pew, the questions must be anticipated out of the mass of experience that the minister has accumulated in dealing with people's doubts. With convincing affirmation, the preacher faces the doubts of life. He does not descend from the ivory tower of spiritual privilege to the level of human imperfection. Rather, he moves about among his people and their thoughts with a sure sense of their doubts and fears and, with the witness of his faith, helps them to rise step by step above the doubts that destroy. He engages their minds and hearts so that they are lifted to new insight and sustaining faith. They are not harangued; they are helped. They are not threatened; they are challenged.

In this process of relation to his hearers, the preacher will lay a strong hold on the positive resources of living that he knows can be accepted as a common ground for moving ahead. Then he will help to clarify the goals of life so that life may be reorganized with more worthy objectives. He will move beyond the past, and the doubts that may so easily be carried along with the past, and step forward with a promise of new lands to be possessed by creative faith. He will point out the paralyzing nature of the doubts that may possess life and indicate that the great ventures of mankind, as well as each individual life, are statements of faith. Parenthood is an affirmation of faith. Education is an expression of faith. Marriage is an investment of self on the basis of faith. Religion is a devotion to values accepted on faith. At every point in life, its finest fruit is grown on the sturdy branches of faith. Yet the fruits are never grown until the branches grow. So the satisfactions of faith are never achieved without an investment of self in the nature of faith.

The three sermons that follow in résumé indicate some of the ways this problem of doubt may be met from the pulpit. With an awareness of the two types of doubting and of the differing sources from which doubts come, they try to give positive programs for action that will neither disappoint the honest doubter nor fortify the fears of the neurotic doubter.

I

First is a sermon that seeks to make faith a demonstrable fact of creative human experience and then to add the element of inspiration that can make faith not only reasonable but desirable and achievable.

FAITH IS TRUER THAN DOUBT

Text: *"Above all, [take] the shield of faith, wherewith ye shall be able to quench all the fiery darts of the wicked."*
—EPH. 6:16

Faith may often be lost, not by active disbelief, but by default. An old house in Vermont, unoccupied for years, was reduced by the elements of nature to a pile of rubble. Lilacs grew up through the porch, and vines, through the windows. Roof and floor fell in. It takes a heap of living in a house to keep it home, and it takes a heap of living in a faith to keep it a useful instrument of life.

Faith is related to a larger view of life. It is not measured by the past but is drawn toward the future, "sustained and soothed by an unfaltering trust." A researcher in telepathy found that subjects who believed in telepathy have a measurably higher score in telepathic tests. Men subjected to strength tests under hypnosis showed a marked physical conditioning to a belief in their strength or weakness. Such also can be true of the quality of faith that sustains life.

Faith, according to Washington Gladden, could be defined as living with an emotional acceptance of those things we give intellectual assent to—by acting as we believe. As we believe, so we become. With faith in life, life becomes more worthy of faith. With faith in self, self is more readily accepted. With faith in God, we can feel more at home in the universe.

While doubt lets life do something to you, faith can do something to life. When doubt puts you in wrong relation to everything else, faith puts you in right relation to life. When doubt denies both God's goodness and love's reality, faith makes a God of love a real pattern for your living. While doubt takes power away from life, faith gives power to it. With faith in self, you become a person more worth believing in. The shield of faith protects from sensitiveness and injury and gives health and vigor to actively combat the disruptive forces that plague all living.

In this sermon, faith is not approached as a theological matter but rather as a vital, active force. It is demonstrated on various levels of experience, and the listener is then challenged to respond to the revelations of faith in his own experience.

II

Starting with the idea that little things can make a great difference, the following sermon deals with the importance of the ideas that hold life together. Faith is such an idea. Doubt becomes denial. Faith becomes fulfillment. In life's various experiences there is need for a creative idea that holds the varied experience in a significant pattern.

THE IDEA THAT HOLDS LIFE TOGETHER

Text: *"I go bound in the spirit unto Jerusalem, not knowing the things that shall befall me."*—ACTS 20:22

A sturdily built old barn of massive hand-hewn timbers fell. The timbers were strong and sound. The foundation was solid and secure. The weakness was in the small wooden pins that held it together. Rain had leaked in and rot destroyed the little things that held the large timbers together. Sometimes ideas seem small or unimportant. But they are the small factors that hold together and give meaning to the large experience of living. Worry, concern, inability to forgive or forget, bickerings, and grudges reflect the decay of faith in self and others which brings rot and collapse to human experience.

By using the principle of the arch, a stone bridge in New Hampshire has been held together for over a hundred years. Without mortar or cement, the stone blocks were secure because of an idea. Through spring freshets and heavy burdens of the years, the bridge gave testimony to the power of an idea. With an adequate idea to hold them together, what may be meaningless blocks of human experience can fit into a useful pattern. Without such an idea, a bridge or a life may become a pile of rubble. Paul, with many and difficult experiences as the raw material of his life, moved beyond doubt and uncertainty to a faith that made him useful and sent him forth in a new spirit, even when he did not know what lay ahead.

To doubt life, makes life doubtful. To believe in a worthy purpose for life, makes life purposeful. Many in our day suffer from the atrophying effect of a small faith or a large doubt. The reverse may be achieved by giving proper place to the seemingly unimportant factors of the ideas that can hold life together. A life that is a mass of frustrating experience, or a useful instrument for a great purpose—the choice is in the hands of those who sense the importance of the ideas that hold life together. Paul found such a principle, but it was not easy. You may do the same, though not easily. The result, however, is worth the effort.

In this sermon the approach and the material are related to human experience as the raw material of life, and the quality of faith is the source of meaning for the raw material. The relation between the experience, the meaning, and the resulting effect upon all of life is stressed. No false assurance is given, but uppermost is the urge to invest one's self in finding life's finest meaning.

III

In the following sermon Halford E. Luccock uses a simple device to center thought on the damaging effect of false ideas upon life. He invites self-examination and a healthy re-evaluation of the idea climate in which we live.

STATIONED IN THE ILLUSIONS [1]

A mother whose son was on military duty off the coast of Alaska informed her neighbor that her son "was stationed in the illusions." Starting from this point, Luccock points out the fact that many persons have unconsciously taken up permanent residence with the type of ideas and experience that are not real.

[1] Adapted from "Stationed in the Illusions," *The Chaplain*. Used by permission.

There are those who have illusory ideas of their own importance. There are those who have false ideas of their place in the universe. There are those who feel that they can get through life taking more out of it than they put into it. There are those who feel that they can escape the consequences of their behavior. There are those who think that they can violate human and moral law with impunity. Such persons live in the illusions.

The only way to get back on the mainland of life is to come to grips with these false ideas. We must get ourselves into focus. We must see ourselves as we are. We must make a gentleman's agreement with life to put more into it than we take out. We must realize that we cannot compartmentalize life, for every part is inseparably related to every other. All experience becomes permanently a part of every one of us. We do not violate moral law; we merely break ourselves against it, even though it may take a long time to realize the fact.

The doubter is prone to build a structure of false ideas about himself and about other people. He also builds false ideas about his relation to God and the universe. He easily makes for himself a cocoon of false security, for doubt builds a house that may destroy itself with its own weight. But the wise learn to doubt their doubts and to penetrate their illusions. They are not satisfied until they see themselves as they are, and others as they are, and God as he is. In fact, the doubter never really learns to live unless he can be transferred from his illusions to a world of reasonable conclusions.

Within the scope of one sermon it is possible to deal with a large number of false ideas about life that may be the stock in trade of the doubter. This sermon shows what such ideas do to the person whose life is bound by them, but it also shows how a person may move beyond the false ideas to more sound ones. It does so in an interesting, amusing, and disarming way, so that persons are not put on the defensive but are urged to smile at their foolishness and correct it.

CHAPTER X

Preaching to the Tense

During a period of relaxation, a physician in a thinly settled rural community spoke candidly of the differences between the kinds of cases discussed in medical school and those he actually encountered in the rural community. He indicated that there are rural diseases which are seldom seen in city practice, and city illnesses that are unknown in rural areas. He supported his statement by pointing out that he had been carefully trained to deal with certain types of heart disease prevalent in cities but had yet to come across such a heart condition in his rural community.

There are good physical and psychological reasons why such differences should be observed. Life in urban areas is physically precarious. Crossing a street is hazardous business. The physical organism is kept at a point of persistent tension by the demands of city living. This state of tension projects itself into the human relations that are a part of city life. It affects eating habits, social relations, and the hurried schedule of activities. Not only that, it is heightened by the noise-creating factors that are always at work. There is no time in the life of a city quite comparable to that period of early morning on a farm, when the symphony of the birds has been completed and the sun is about to burst over the horizon. The majestic calmness that presides at the moment of the creation of a new day is not only impressive in and of itself, but it does things to the lives of those who are a part of it. How different is that moment of calm majesty from the jarring rattle of an alarm clock, the hurried breakfast in an atmosphere of confusion, the rush for a train which rattles and roars its way into the maelstrom of noise and congestion that is a modern city! It is little wonder that the hearts of men who live in a city are affected by tension-creating conditions. Yet without the right attitude toward life, the farmer may not value his freedom from tension and, in boredom, may revert to the jug of applejack.

Nor is it the heart alone that shows this effect. The environment of noise and congestion for which man was not created may take its toll of that portion of the person which first shows any signs of weakness. The individual with a strong heart may reveal his tension through digestive disturbance. Others may show no physical symptoms but will increasingly reveal their tension through disturbed human relations, quick temper, argumentativeness, and aggressive behavior. Still others will seek to escape the tensions that are a part of life by withdrawal, drinking, and other available types of escape. Sometimes it seems that the large crop of high fidelity devotees that has sprung up in recent years is prompted not so much by a genuine love of fine music as by a desperate desire to blot out the discordant noises with a quality and quantity of sound that is harmonious and beautiful.

Those who minister to urban parishes must always be aware of this mood of tension that exists among their parishioners. Many come to church with a desire to find a respite from the tension-creating factors about them. While it is not the primary mission of the preacher to treat indigestion, colitis, high blood pressure, heart disease, and upper respiratory infections, he cannot escape a responsibility for dealing with the life factors that disturb his people. Tenseness has never been designated as one of the cardinal sins, but from the point of view of its life-destroying potential it cannot be ignored. The problems that develop in marriage, child-parent relations, community good will, and personal adjustment cannot be separated easily from this relatively new factor that has been projected into life by modern conditions. Nor can the preacher fail to deal with it. If he is to be genuinely helpful he must furnish some of the antidotes to tension that can help his people to live effectively in spite of their physical environment.

As the custodian of traditional religious concepts and practices, he can give practical suggestions. The family altar is such a suggestion. Instead of grabbing the newspaper in the morning to cram the mind with the latest human horrors and catastrophes, the individual and the family may help to create the pattern for the day's thinking by making a quiet time to contemplate the deep inner recesses of the soul, with its capacity for calm relatedness to the spiritual power of the universe. The calm attitude instituted by a pattern of prayer can emphasize the spiritual nature of life at the beginning of the day in such a way that all of the activities of that day are flavored by it. Similarly, at the end of the day one can be prepared for peaceful sleep by the mood of prayer that entrusts life to the great and calm peace which only God can give.

When Leslie Weatherhead preached to his blitz-harassed congregation in wartime London, he used the psychologist's knowledge of word function. He produced at the time a volume of sermons called *The Significance of Silence*. From the studies of psychologists into linguistics, he well knew that the relation of words to mental attitudes and physical responses is a primitive and often unexplainable reaction. Frequently the very act of saying a word does things to the person who hears it. As Ernst Cassirer has pointed out in his *Essay on Man,* the very nature of

111

thought is inseparably related to words that can be articulated. And contrary to general opinion there is no such thing as silent or unarticulated thought, for the very thinking of a word has muscular counterparts even though they may not be traceable in audible expression. The person who is paralyzed so that certain areas of human speech are no longer possible has a comparable difficulty in dealing with the concepts that the words suggest. If this is true of a form of paralysis, it may also be true of that form of atrophy that develops when certain words and concepts are allowed to lapse through neglect and disuse. The preacher can bring an active therapeutic force into the tensed lives of his people by saying certain words and illustrating them effectively. This may seem to turn preaching into a type of magical mumbo jumbo. But here we are dealing with demonstrable principles of human thought. The power to suggest attitudes and actions is the first step in the influence of one personality over another through hypnosis. Certain types of highly emotional preaching are chracterized by much repetition and a rhythm of word and phrase. Its effectiveness is not so much a matter of an appeal to thought and reason as it is a stimulation of emotional response by calculated use of what might be called "trigger" words and phrases. Aware of the same emotional responses but using them at a different level, the discerning preacher may bring concepts to life in the minds and hearts of his listeners by skillfully using a constellation of word relationships and meanings.

Harry Emerson Fosdick has long been aware of this power of words in his approach to the persons of a large city. In his sermon "Be Still and Know," he uses a skillful relationship of the words and phrases that cultivate a concept of creative silence as the basis for a sensitivity of spirit. When the noise and confusion of city life may so project itself into the personality of the city dweller that the very concept of stillness and quiet may be allowed to die of disuse, the preacher has the responsibility to keep that concept a vital part of life experience. Sermons on prayer, meditation, silence, and beauty may help to vitalize the concept. While it may seem that it is paradoxical to create the concept of silence by the use of words in the preaching function, nevertheless it is a demonstrable force at work in the mind of the hearer. The concept of silence may be made alive by the skillful cultivation of the word-suggested and word-related moods and concepts. Perhaps more than has ever been realized, this rather recently established fact of communication explains much of the power that preaching has exerted over the lives of people down through the years. This very instrument that the preacher uses from week to week is a powerful force for therapy. Though he may not have understood all that was involved, the very response of people to it through generations has verified its power and kept it alive as an instrument of healing. Now that it is better understood, the responsibility for a careful and skillful use of it rests more consciously upon him.

Harry Stack Sullivan, in his research into the nature of symbolism and its effect upon human thought, has clarified this matter. The idea of primary, secondary, and tertiary symbolism is not easy to grasp, but it is significant for our approach to the minds of people. Language itself is a mass of primary symbols. A word stands for an experience and suggests it. In that sense it is an abstraction and a symbol. But the word "cow" immediately suggests a real, and mentally visible, concrete image. We see a cow. The word "cow" represents a primary symbol. However, we deal with a different level of mental activity when we hear that two and two are four. Here we deal with secondary abstractions, for the words are abstracts for the primary abstracts that may ultimately be made concrete. Two and two may be, but do not necessarily have to be, two apples and two oranges. But this

113

process of abstraction is raised to a third level when we speak of the immortality of the soul, for here we are dealing with abstracts for which there is no ultimate concrete reality. Language then becomes a matter of abstractions about the ultimate abstractions.

Since much of preaching deals with such ultimate abstractions, it necessarily moves often at the third level of abstract communication. Here the mind of the listener may be very much at the mercy of the mind of the speaker, for the concepts are in effect created as they are used. The preacher who uses this powerful force over the minds of other persons without a careful evaluation of the cause-effect relationship of his utterance is apt to be playing fast and loose with the sensitive nature of human personality. In a very real sense he is engaged in creating the mind of his listeners. He should be well aware of the nature and direction of his action. The last few years have placed a heavy sense of responsibility upon the personal counselor and the psychotherapist for words spoken to a listening individual. Those who have the privilege of speaking to groups should entertain a comparable concern about the nature of their use of words as they affect the minds of individuals in a listening group.

It is humbling to contemplate the magic of words. No preacher has been at his task long without feeling an almost unaccountable response from his people when he deals with certain types of communicated thought. For instance, a preacher may use scripture to that end. Certain well-known verses may be especially helpful to the tensed person. "Peace I leave with you, my peace I give unto you: not as the world giveth, give I unto you. Let not your heart be troubled, neither let it be afraid." (John 14:27.) Such a quotation brings a response in a number of minds that react to emotional stimuli. To say, "Come unto me all ye that labour and are heavy laden, and I will give you rest" (Matt. 11:

28), tends to create an immediate mood of response. So the preacher, in dealing with persons tensed by the circumstances of life, has it in his power to say the words and stimulate the thoughts which, more than he realizes, may become an antidote for the life-destroying tensions of his day. But to do it with skill and understanding becomes a matter of specific concern for him.

The preacher then becomes a therapist able to help create the mood within which his people can learn to relax. He can help them to carry more adequately the burdens that seem unbearable. Like the farmer who fits the yoke to his shoulders to distribute the weight of the maple sap buckets, so the preacher uses the words which may stimulate the thoughts that will help his listeners to distribute the weight of their burdens. He can help persons to see themselves more adequately in relation to their work load so that they will be content to do one thing at a time and try to do only what is reasonable. He can help his hearers to relax and adjust to life as they see the importance of being kind to themselves at the point of the unreasonable demands that they may often make upon self. He is also concerned about emphasizing the values that relate to life, for he is communicating the idea that it is not primarily how much you bear but how you carry it that counts. He isolates the tensions that tire and brings to the level of active consciousness the capacity for relaxation that truly rests.

While this process of helping people to relax may not itself be a matter of great spiritual insight, it may become the basis upon which that insight can be built. The preacher may well define the nature and importance of physical relaxation as it relates to mental relaxation and spiritual peace, for all of these are interwoven in the rest of living. Many of the human problems that are most disturbing might well be eased by learning to handle the more specific tensions that create the lesser effects.

In the three sermons that follow, the preachers approach the problem of the tensions of life positively by presenting the antidotes that are readily accessible to their hearers. With a clear concern for spiritual values, they proceed to make available the mental and emotional furnishing that can give specific aid in dealing with the forces of modern life which diffuse energy and destroy the functional integrity of the personality.

I

In this sermon Leslie Weatherhead creates the mood for emotional response in addition to furnishing the intellect with the concepts that encourage creative organization of the thought life about health-giving ideas. He does not avoid difficult problems but faces them directly, with the values that can fortify the personality as it deals with its own needs.

THE SIGNIFICANCE OF SILENCE [1]
Text: *"Study to be quiet."*—I Thess. 4:11

Silence is significant in moments of exultation. A vacation, a vision of beauty, an experience of spiritual satisfaction, call for a period of deep silence in order to realize the full responsibilities of the joy. We must often create the mood where the "still small voice" can be heard. The Quakers were wise in sensing the importance of silence for the soul's growth. We cannot let the significance of such creative silence escape us.

Silence is significant at the hour of the soul's grief. When Jesus heard of the death of his close friend, John the Baptist, he did not preach a sermon on immortality or the nature of human suffering. He asked his disciples to go with him into a desert place and be alone. Here in the silence that is related to eternal things, perspective can

---

[1] Adapted from the title sermon in *The Significance of Silence* (New York and Nashville: Abingdon Press, 1945). Used by permission.

116

be rebuilt. Grief that is deep calls for that silence which encourages the communication of deep with deep.

Silence is also important in the hour of the soul's refusal to come to grips with reality. Jesus readily sensed the time when words served no purpose. When at the trials he was mocked, he knew that the minds of his hearers or accusers were closed and words were useless. When he was ridiculed upon the cross he knew that an answer was of no avail. He kept that silence out of which could come the understanding of such a prayer as "Father, forgive."

We may escape much of life's meaning by stopping thinking, or we may take time to stop and think. We can make room for silence in life and use that time to prepare our souls for life's joys or tragedies. "Study to be quiet."

Using a careful psychological progression, the preacher starts with the experiences of joy and the soul's exultation. This is essential preparation for the rest of life's experience. Then he moves on to speak of the experience that is most real to his war-immersed listeners, that of grief and the deep injustice which cannot be answered by words, but only by a quietness within that can teach the mood of the prayer of forgiveness. Here is spiritual affirmation that is honest, real, and courageous, fortifying the depths of the soul.

II

In the following sermon the preacher tries to help people plan for the type of vacation experience that will restore their spirits as well as their bodies. As tenseness may begin in a mental attitude so it may be overcome at the level of the mind's relaxation.

MAKING THE MOST OF YOUR VACATION
Text: *"Come ye . . . apart . . . a while."*—MARK 6:31

During the summer many of you will be enjoying a vacation. You will plan pleasant experiences in interesting places. It is well

117

to plan to meet the needs of your total being. Tiredness often begins in the mind. Fatigue is often a matter of the spirit. To fail to take these matters into account may mean that your vacation will not serve its largest purpose.

We need strength for living in perilous times, but this strength is not essentially physical. More and more persons are using their summers for the type of spiritual retreat that restores the soul and brings clearer spiritual meaning to life. "The Camp Farthest Out" and Ashrams patterned after the Indian retreats of E. Stanley Jones are exerting increasing influence on the spiritual lives of people. Summer camping experiences sponsored by the church bring this opportunity to thousands of our people, young and old. It is a creative approach to the effect of tensions on the total life of the person.

Man is more than an accident. As a God-conscious person he is not at ease until his soul is related to God. A vacation may be a creative spiritual experience as well as a time of escape. When it is the former, all of life is made more adequate for the tasks that are ahead. As you prepare for your vacation, do not ignore the more important needs of your life, but heed the admonition of the Master to "come ye . . . apart . . . a while" for spiritual growth.

In this sermon a direct approach is made to the listener to use that portion of time usually set aside for relaxation, for the type that takes into account the needs of mind and soul. The sermon also relates the religious resources available to help meet the need. It is not only a word to the tense but may well become a way out for them as well.

III

At Riverside Church Harry Emerson Fosdick preached continually to the people who were immersed in the life of a great city. In the sermon used here he was speaking during a great financial depression. One has the feeling that he is plumbing depths of the spirit which most of his listeners must have forgotten they possessed. Combining psychological understanding, intellectual mastery, and inspiration, the sermon must have lifted the souls of those who heard it.

BE STILL AND KNOW
Text: *"Be still, and know that I am God."*—Ps. 46:10

Much evil and unhappiness arise from our inability to be still. This is not sentimentality but the evidence of modern life. The life that is truly productive draws from the depths of quiet contemplation. The engineer, the artist, the poet, and the scientist recognize the need to be still. Creativity is "the harvest of the quiet eye."

People who are perpetually in a noisy hustle usually make life awry for themselves and those about them. How many family quarrels would be creatively handled if instead of the thunder and lightning, there was a quiet talk!

The life of the spirit is always dependent upon this response from the quiet depths. Elijah heard the "still small voice"; you will not learn to handle your own lives until you too can listen in quietness.

Even the insight needed for creative social life demands quiet. One does not stand for justice unless he has let the nature of injustice reach into the quiet recesses of his soul. True religion is not so much a matter of noise as it is of silence that precedes action.

Einstein indicates that the heart of religiousness is "to wonder and stand rapt in awe." In that sense the modern scientist is akin to the ancient prophet. The noisy critics come and go but those who create in quietness build for the centuries.

Busyness and noisiness become enemies of religious growth. We need to learn again the art of being still, for in such times of quiet searching we come to know God and the meaning of our living.

In this sermon the wonders of the spiritual life are presented so logically and winsomely that the hearer takes a new value for his own soul and sets about developing the spiritual resources which can take the destructiveness out of his disquieted living.

CHAPTER XI

Preaching to the Sick and Shut-in

The Church has always felt a strong responsibility for those who are ill. Jesus in his ministry gave special attention to the physically sick and the mentally disturbed. Down through the ages the Church has been instrumental in instituting both new concerns and new techniques for dealing with the temporarily or chronically indisposed. Each new generation seems to have afforded new opportunities for the expression of this concern and for the employment of specialized techniques toward healing.

Within the past fifty years or less two very important factors in the church's ministry to the sick have developed. One is the increased use of hospitals for treating illness and the other is the radio and TV communication. A major portion of those with serious illness are now treated in hospitals, and many of these institutions have either part-time or full-time chaplain's service. The new means of communication afforded by radio and TV make it possible for the pulpit message to be carried to an ever increasing number of sickrooms, so that as never before, the word is preached to all in divers conditions.

A great deal has been done to guide the preacher in his personal ministry to those who are sick. Valuable handbooks have been prepared with instructions and guidance for the individualized bedside ministry. Small pamphlets for the special use of the ill are available for distribution. Competent studies of the most effective methods for counseling the ill have been prepared by the best minds working in the field. Yet very little has been done to guide the minister who has the responsibility for preaching to the sick, either directly or indirectly.

In the rather limited space allotted in the following paragraphs there are indicated some of the principles that may guide the pastor who is obliged to preach to the sick. While it is recognized that there are persons in the congregation every Sunday who harbor one or another type of illness, this chapter does not deal with them. Here the effort is made to indicate how preaching may be used as a therapeutic instrument in the environment of the hospital or in other places where the majority of the hearers are sick. The hospital chaplain has a special congregation and a clearly defined task. The preacher whose sermons are carried via radio must always be aware of the large number of sickrooms into which his message goes.

At the beginning it is important to indicate that, for the person who is ill, the other parts of the service may be more important than the sermon itself. Many persons have said that under such conditions they would listen to the pastoral prayer and then shut off the radio. They did not have the strength nor the inclination to deal with the longer sermon but found in the prayer of the pastor an utterance of reassurance, an expression of faith, a source of strength for the day, and a guide to the troubled. Under conditions where the sick may hear, it may be a good practice never to pray without making a specific effort to relate the prayer to their needs. We know that there is healing power in prayer. We have witnessed it many times in the sickroom. We cannot let the opportunity of public prayer pass without special petitions for the doctors, nurses, and others who co-operate in the healing ministry. Nor should we forget to mention those who are physically or emotionally ill. The careful choice of hymns and readings from the Scriptures may also help to serve a real need of the sick.

Preaching to the sick presents a set of physical circumstances quite different from usual preaching. Worries, concerns, and needs are different. Because of that the special religious opportunities are unusually significant. Special needs have a way of making the soul fertile for the word that is carefully chosen.

The hospital chapel presents one type of opportunity. Here are persons who have come because they wanted to. One has more freedom in speaking to them than would be possible through the use of a general public-address system. Usually these are persons who are convalescing or are preparing for surgery. Often persons facing an operation are apprehensive or depressed. Many physicians refuse to operate on a person in a state of depression. The type of circumstantial depression that may come upon a person in a preoperative period is usually superficial and can be remedied by a more creative sense of perspective or a deepening of the roots of faith. Often the mood of a person can be changed by words spoken by the understanding and effective hospital chaplain. At other times the message may serve to open the door for counseling so that the fears or guilt feelings disturbing the patient can be more adequately examined. Others attending the chapel services may be convalescing. Here the problem is likely to be restlessness, impatience, concern about the finances involved in hospitalization, or readjustment to life in a more limited mode of existence. Here again a new sense of perspective and a new grip on eternal values can sustain the patient. In any event the sermon should be short, simple in language, and positive in emphasis, for it is easy to tax the strength of persons in such conditions.

There are some hospitals that broadcast the service of worship through ward speakers and individual headphones. Persons may take off their headphones but must endure the loud-speaker. In most instances it is wise to avoid any controversial or denominational utterance, which might further disturb the ill. Often the musical part of the service can be increased and the spoken parts decreased; for there is healing power in fine religious music, and the many recordings now available make it possible to bring the best of sacred music into such use. Such general services may use inspirational poetry, helpful prayers, and scripture readings with rather short devotional messages, using narrative material, which is easier to follow. Perhaps it is good to set a limit of five minutes on any spoken part of such a service, with two or three minutes of interpretation preferable.

In dealing with those who are mentally ill it is important to choose even the music with care. Certain hymns that make reference to the blood of our Lord are emotionally disturbing to some patients and should be omitted. Usually the calm, devout type of hymn is preferable to the kind that appeals to the superficial emotions.

While it often seems that the message of the Christian faith is irrelevant in a hospital filled with the mentally ill, a deeper examination of its content makes the message particularly significant for such sufferers. Religious worship is concerned with wholeness, and the undergirding of life with healthy emotional responses cannot be separated from a firm grasp upon those central aspects of Christian faith. However, these cannot usually be presented effectively in theological form. Rather do we find a clue in the simple narrative technique used by Jesus in the parables. He dealt with great religious truths in terms of easily grasped symbolic speech. There is a wealth of symbolic material available to the preacher even in dealing with those whose illness is mental. He never knows when one of the symbols of security or triumph over difficulty may become the rallying point about which a troubled personality can begin the process of rebuilding healthy attitudes or feelings.

While all of the preceding is relevant to the radio and TV preacher, there are other factors that he will have to consider as well. He is speaking to both the sick and the well. His inclination is to direct his message to those who sit before him, without a special concern for the larger number of sick and shut-in who are always a part of his congregation. It takes a certain type of discipline to prepare a message with this large and unseen audience clearly in mind. They may be desperately seeking some word to cling to, to keep them through another day. Their suffering may seem more than they can bear. Their fears may seem more than they can cope with. It is important for them that each service—either in prayer, scripture, or sermon—have some word that can give them the hope and courage they need to keep going.

It is at this point that some of the traditional emphases of the evangelists may be anxiety-producing and threatening. When a person is ill and upset he is in no condition to deal with a harangue on the subject, "Are you ready to meet your Maker?" While it is important to think constructively of death, it is unwise to use it as a threat to achieve an emotional response. The stock in trade of those who dwell on calamity and its twin, catastrophe, may serve its purpose in some remote places, but it is seldom the message designed to help the ill find courage and strength to face their immediate problem.

It is to be hoped that the messages finding their way into the unseen sickroom will be focused on that soul-sustaining food which is so much a part of true religion. The sick are usually anxious enough without having anyone add to it. They are burdened with their own problems and in no condition to have to wrestle with the problems of the world. This situation is often a taxing discipline of the radio or TV preacher but the responsibility goes with the privilege. His message needs always to be aware of those who come to him for guidance, for courage, and for strength. He must not violate that need.

As always it is important to study the methods Jesus used in speaking to the sick and afflicted. His was always a message of direct, positive faith. He assumed that health and wholeness were the natural states and worked to restore people to that condition. He always assumed that there was a direct relationship between the health of their bodies and the welfare of their spirits. Yet he never dealt with the problems of men as if the laws of nature or of health were to be treated lightly. He adhered closely to a respect for law and order, cause and effect. The attitude expressed during his temptation was expressed all through his life. He felt that spiritual wholeness was an achievement, and he sought to open the way for the insight that made the achievement possible. He preached no pollyanna religion. He saw the place for suffering and even a Cross. His message to the ill was able to give a perspective that could lead the way to wholeness of spirit even if wholeness of body was never possible. He never merely healed people. He helped them to the place where their faith could make them whole. Yet even when physical wholeness was not possible, he had a message of God's redeeming love that made men spiritually whole and thus adequate for whatever the physical incidents of life would bring them. His was not a message of denial. Rather, it was one of spiritual fulfillment.

Modern scientific insight into the nature of illness and the psychogenic nature of much physical disturbance goes far to increase the status of the spoken ministry as an instrument of health. It also increases the responsibility of those who use the spoken word with the ill, to employ it in such a way that it fulfills its purpose and does not become an added source of confusion, guilt, anxiety, and ill health. One cannot be too well informed about the relationship between the condition of the spirit and its effect upon health. Neither can one lose sight of the fact that, although health and religious wholeness are related, there is also a time when physical illness may help to bring health of spirit. The wise preacher is always aware of both possibilities.

The following three sermons may help to illustrate the types that can be used, with modifications in length, in speaking to the sick.

I

Often the difference between recovery and continued illness is a matter of attitude. Harry Emerson Fosdick deals directly with such a matter in this sermon, which is concerned with what we do with what happens to us.

GETTING THE BEST OUT OF THE WORST [1]
Text: *"Passing through the valley of Weeping they make it a place of springs."*—Ps. 84:6 (A.S.V.)

Life is fraught with difficult experiences. The real problem is not so much why they exist but what we are making of them. Most people sincerely want to know how they can be part of the solution rather than part of the problem.

What makes it possible for some persons to deal constructively with their problems while others go to pieces before them? Temperament is involved and circumstances have their effect. But beyond that there are those made better and those made worse by the same circumstance. Why?

Isaiah took bitterness and translated it into hope. But he first disciplined himself and practiced the art of hope. Abraham Lincoln waded through bitterness and saw a land of hope and promise. He

---

[1] Adapted from "Getting the Best Out of the Worst" in *A Great Time to Be Alive* (New York: Harper & Bros., 1944). Used by permission.

schooled himself through long and sorrow-filled years to seek the humanly hopeful.

Those who work to develop spiritual power are undergirded to meet life's experience, not in terms of the experience alone, but in terms of a deeper meaning for life that turns even difficulty to good ends. Spiritual adequacy spells the difference in dealing with circumstance.

Illness and depression often go hand in hand. Recovery and depression are incompatible. The spiritual resources that can overcome depression are available to those who see a purpose to life that is larger than the various circumstances that make up life. These resources are not mysterious. Rather, they are the achievement of the disciplined soul. It requires effort to change the point of view but it can be done and it is worth the effort. This sermon points the way toward a larger measure of health and happiness by indicating the way to the spiritual resources that make the difference between personal defeat and personal victory over life circumstance.

II

True religion has always been involved in a struggle to protect the values of the spiritual life in a world that is continually making assaults upon them. The next sermon deals with that struggle and the resources for victory.

ON KEEPING YOUR HEARTS AND MINDS
Text: *"Think on these things."* —PHIL. 4:8

Life in the early church was not easy. Life was filled with trials from without and bickerings from within. St. Paul writes his followers with simple, sound advice.

To keep your mind and heart in a state of health, try to give first place in your thoughts to the positive values of life. How easily we let our minds come to dwell on the disturbing and the painful. Then life takes on the flavor of our thoughts.

There is so much that is true, honest, just, pure, lovely, of good report, virtuous, and praiseworthy, that we can work toward health of mind and spirit by giving it first place in our thoughts. Then we can help to restore life to its proper perspective.

Then the promise can be fulfilled that the "peace of God shall be with you."

The wise person makes a deliberate effort to marshal the forces of the spirit that can deal with depression, gloom, foreboding, and despair. He sets himself the task of cultivating the faith that sustains life by dwelling on the positive values that can be seen and cultivated. Such a sermon can leave one simple thought. It can be compressed into but a minute or two of time, as may fit the occasion in the hospital situation. But the message is positive and health giving, even if brief.

III

In this next sermon we face the problem of cowardice and bravery in the common experiences of life. We look at the inadequate approaches to those situations which are not of our asking but are thrust upon us.

STAND FAST IN THE FAITH

Text: *"For a great door . . . is opened unto me, and there are many adversaries."*—I COR. 16:9

Doors open to opportunity and to responsibility at the same time. The two seem to go together always.

Even illness and life tragedy can be door-opening experiences. Much is determined by the attitude of mind and the quality of faith that the person takes with him into the life experience.

Bravery can be interpreted as an ability to stand fast. This does not mean that the brave are not fearful. They are, but they are not so possessed by their fear that they cannot function wisely and well. The brave are able to stand, look life in the eye, and "having done all, to stand." Bravery has a quality of unmovable firmness about it. As its faith is sure, so is its action.

All adventure involves hardship. Gethsemane was an open door but it was also an adversary. Self-will is always in conflict with God's will. Often the adversary is within the life of the individual. We can learn to stand fast in a faith that opens doors of opportunity and is not easily defeated by the adversaries that come with opened doors.

Out of our own experience we build the concept of the courage that is related to a higher fate. What the coward curses the brave man uses. The power of God to bring healing understanding to life is a resource that can stimulate bravery in the face of a persistent circumstance that is disheartening. This sermon should bring courage to the ill and discouraged as well as stiffen the spine of those who may be in danger of flinching, and having brought courage it may well help to restore a measure of health.

CHAPTER XII

Preaching to Those Who Feel Inferior

One of the first psychological terms to be generally accepted and used was "the inferiority complex." It seemed that in some direct way this phrase kindled a response in the minds of many persons who felt that they understood what such a phrase should mean. Apart from any specific or detailed understanding of the factors that are at work to make a complex, these persons felt that it described them and their feelings. Perhaps this phrase gave a needed handle for that feeling many persons have about their own inadequacy in the face of social demands that seem too great and competitive forces that are too demanding. Sometimes persons escape into a phrase rather than accept the discipline of understanding what is needed to rise above it.

It is reasonable to believe that there will be numerous persons within the congregation each Sunday who have a feeling of personal inadequacy. They undoubtedly come to find something to sustain them in the day's work. Just as the obsessive-compulsive neurotic is continually looking for some kind of an external, rigid framework to shore up the structure of his personality, so the person with feelings of inferiority is seeking some emotional support that can help him through the duties of another week.

But in order to deal effectively with the needs of such persons it is important to try to understand why they have such needs.

These feelings of inadequacy may be deep rooted in the experience of childhood. Early comparisons with other children may have made them feel inadequate. Early emotional attitudes of their parents may have given them the feeling that they were not wanted. Childhood experiences such as illness or long hospitalization may have given them a feeling of separation and a lack of personal competence. Such episodes create the backlog of emotions about which a complex of inferiority feelings can grow.

Sometimes the difficult years of adolescence produce the feelings that become a damaging part of the personality structure. During this period of normal neurosis when the personality is trying to learn to deal with new and strong impulses, any social injury or defeat may quickly become a major determinant of future attitude. The boy who is seeking social recognition through athletics may be seriously injured by the spontaneous groan from the crowd that witnesses his error at a strategic point in the game. The crowd may quickly forget, but the youth may not forget the defeat and failure that he feels. The relatively weak ego force of the adolescent may receive a shock so strong that the rest of life may show the marks of it. Who knows how many criminals are trying to establish their courage, or how many hermits are trying to separate themselves forever from the society that has inflicted deadly injury upon their souls!

Some of the symptoms of inferiority feelings are readily discernible. Timidity and shyness are more easily understood than the extreme aggressiveness that is an effort to obscure the feelings of inadequacy. The desire to be always in the limelight may be an effort to escape being ignored. The overdramatic may well be an effort to compensate inferiority feelings.

The Casper Milquetoast, the extremely underassertive personality, may be showing inferiority feelings that are comparable in nature to the person who, with booming voice and assertive ways, barges into the center of every group. The worker in the church who will never say "no" to any request but will work himself inordinately to achieve some recognition from the pastor may be just as much involved with inferiority feelings as the person who is always excusing himself because he feels he does not have enough ability to do anything. The soprano who always wants to sing solos even though her lack of talent is evident to everyone else may be showing the lack of reality sense that is often evident among those with deep inferiority feelings which are always driving them toward unreasonable compensation. The boisterous drinker may be dealing with the same feeling of inferiority that is shown by the superficially pious person who is always seeking to win approbation for his saintly patience and forbearance.

Sometimes these same feelings may be camouflaged by an attitude of aggressive manliness. A man may try to turn his wife into a mother substitute by making her wait on him hand and foot. While he may think it is the dominance of his masculine nature, she may realize that it is his regression to a childhood state of dependence upon his mother. Because he has found himself to be inadequate for the responsibilities of adult life, he makes an emotional home for his injured personality in a world of fantasy where his wife is made to serve a mother's function.

Sometimes this living in a world of fantasy can become so extreme that the personality ceases to function effectively in other phases of living and we have the more complicated manifestations of a "nervous breakdown." The dynamics of the nervous breakdown often involve a major retreat of the personality to a state of dependence upon others because of a feeling of inadequacy at the point of specifically accepted responsibilities. A preacher may find himself faced with strong emotions that make it impossible for him to preach, or a teacher feels unable to face a class of students, or an actress unable to walk out upon the stage. Such feelings are a signal for at least a temporary retreat into circumstances that guarantee the personality a larger measure of security until he is again able to cope with the problems of his life.

In dealing with such a variety of manifestations of the feeling of inferiority, the pastor can play an important function through the effective use of pulpit utterance. He can help to prevent the acute form of manifestation of these feelings. He can encourage an adjustive relationship to such feelings. He can carry on an active program of helping personalities to so understand their own feelings and the source of them that corrective action can be taken.

To interpret to parents the nature and cause of psychic trauma, or soul injury, may make it possible to prevent some of the conditions in childhood that would cause feelings of inferiority. Such a purpose is well within the range of traditional pulpit utterance, especially at such times as Children's Day, Religious Education Day, and services for baptism.

The adjustive function in preaching may deal specifically with the need for developing a sympathetic and responsive attitude toward those who are bothered by inferiority feelings. So often, a careless remark or a thoughtless attitude may be particularly injurious to those who already have a low measure of self-esteem. Also an understanding of causes may make possible a wiser relation to effects. The hypochondriac is not nearly so much in need of more sympathy as he is of a more understanding attitude toward his basic emotional state. Unwise sympathy may only fortify his false attitudes toward himself. The same would be true of the person whose feelings of inferiority had been responsible for an inadequate reality sense. He needs to see things as they are rather than have others fortify his illusions by indicating that they share his views. To be able to carry on a wise adjustive relationship to the emotions of the disturbed may serve to bring them to a more healthy understanding of their own needs.

But the corrective function of the pulpit may be most rewarding. While it is important to recognize that problems rising from unconscious states or from those deep subconscious states will not be responsive to a direct approach and therefore need special treatment, it is reasonable to believe that many of those cases that grow from wrong adjustments and false ideas can be corrected by an approach to the minds and emotions of the hearer.

Self-knowledge can be an important element in self-correction. More than we realize, persons are doing this all the time. Most persons who are able to function effectively in their human relations are continually bringing themselves and their behavior into focus so that they may correct it. To see themselves as they are is important, and the sermon is well within its traditional function when it invites self-examination and analysis. A young officer who had been a college instructor was in command of a difficult army outpost in a foreign country. Though morale had been low he seemed to have few problems after he took over the outfit. When once he was asked about his success with his men he pointed to a full-length mirror on the wall. At the top printed in letters so small that one had to get close to read it was the question, "Proud of yourself?" The officer indicated that he seldom had to reprimand any of his men further than asking them to read that question. Then they paused to look at themselves full-length. They had to look themselves squarely in the eye. That was usually enough to bring the needed insight and changed behavior.

The sermon can be an instrument to bring people face to face with themselves and their feelings. The life and the personality of Christ can be used as the mirror within which people can see themselves and their possibilities more clearly. They can understand the inadequacy of their feelings about themselves and the value of their life because they can see that it has a value in the sight of God so important that the witness of Christ could be made in its behalf.

Where there is low self-esteem through a sense of guilt, the healing, redeeming love of God can be revealed as the source of new life and new values and a new estimate of self. Where low esteem and feelings of inadequacy are the result of early childhood experience, a person can be given a perspective to help him move beyond the distant past. He can be brought to see the importance and integrity of every soul and the important elements of individuality in every creature. Then the injurious effects of past comparisons may be relieved. When a person is afraid to be himself but is always trying to copy others and live in reflected glory, he can have the values of the best self so clearly indicated that he will see the undeveloped possibilities within himself and will work toward their realization.

So often we see the tragedy of those who sell themselves short. They put a price tag upon themselves that is much below what is warranted. The pulpit can be an instrument in helping to place a more adequate value upon each person as a child of God. After preaching a Reformation Day sermon on the priesthood of every soul, the pastor was approached by a woman who said that for the first time in her life she felt that her ideas and judgments might be of real value. As a child of a broken home she had spent the early years of life with relatives and had evidently never come to feel that she really belonged to anyone or anything. Her response to such a sermon was unusual but, for her, quite real since at last she had gained a sense of belonging to the Reformation Church as a soul with a direct relation and a real value to God.

Religion has an important message to those who hold themselves in low esteem. They are important in the family of God. Their ideas are real before God and their struggle to find life's meaning is a struggle which has the elements of a divine partnership. The sermon may be an effective instrument in bringing knowledge of self and healing adjustment to the more important self that may be released.

The sermon outlines that follow indicate how the pulpit has been used to speak directly to those with low self-esteem, in an effort to bring to their lives a more realistic concept of self and a more vital energy in realizing the potential within their own lives.

I

The first sermon is biographical in nature. It follows the experiences of a person who had to overcome severe feelings of inadequacy to become one of the great leaders of human history. An effort is made to keep the material so narrative in nature that the hearers will engage their own emotions in the process and arrive at a new estimate of their own resources.

HANDLING FEELINGS OF INFERIORITY
Text: Exodus 3

The life of Moses had the marks of an uncertain childhood. His loyalties were confused. Though given privileges of education, he never realized quite where he belonged or to what his loyalty should be given. His uncertainty broke forth in aggressive action and he was compelled to run away. His life was in danger. He had foolishly resorted to violence. He felt broken in spirit and defeated by the failure of his efforts. He became almost a hermit in primitive surroundings, from prince to pauper in one short scene.

But deep within he was not satisfied. He wrestled with the God-consciousness within himself. He could not ignore, though he tried to deny, the demands of God upon his life. He became aware of the presence of God and took off his shoes in worship. But still he could not agree to be a spokesman for God.

He tried to excuse himself, to deny his ability, to withdraw from his responsibility. But at every point he was met by the argument of God. Even when he declared that he could not speak effectively, God said he would fill his mouth with the proper words at the proper time. Under the compulsion of a great cause and a loyalty beyond himself, he went back to do a great work of leadership with patience and understanding.

He moved from violence to self-control, from confusion to certainty, from low self-esteem to useful living, when he moved beyond his own small problems to devotion to his people and his God. So the conquest of petty preoccupation with self and the dominance of low esteem is always related to a will beyond the self, a cause larger than self, an active relationship to the source of great spiritual power, God himself.

In such a sermon, principles of spiritual living are not described or theorized about. They are illustrated in human experience. The concentration on the life and experience of one person gives a good basis for the self-involvement of the listener. Where his feelings parallel the feelings of the narrative, he cannot avoid becoming engaged in an active emotional response. This may be carried through to more healthy self-realization.

II

In the following sermon résumé Henry Hitt Crane indicates how the individual can be encouraged to face his weaknesses and inadequacies. By emphasizing the quality of the "valiant," both strength and worth can be brought to life activity. It makes persons dissatisfied with their own inadequate self-judgments by helping them face the judgment that God would place upon their behavior.

137

VALIANT BEHAVIOR [1]

Text: *"Be of good courage, and let us behave ourselves valiantly for our people, and for the cities of our God; and let the Lord do that which is good in his sight."*—I CHR. 19:13

Life's basic problem is related to behavior. How can we behave like the person responsive to God? How can we establish motives equal to the demands of circumstance? The Old Testament story of Hanun's suspicious reaction to David's expression of sympathy at the death of Hanun's father Nahash, is used to indicate the effect of circumstance that can plague life.

There are times when valiant behavior seems to be all that is left. To be valiant is to be stouthearted, intrepid in danger, creatively courageous, modestly meritorious, inwardly invincible, eventually victorious. David's general called on his troops in the words of the text. They had not chosen the circumstance of treachery, but they were not going to capitulate through weakness. The spiritual implication is clear—be valiant, do your best, and rest confident through faith in God.

The great contributions of the Jewish race have been rooted in this valiant behavior—the personality of Jesus, the Sacred Scriptures. Military victory was secondary to a quality of spiritual life, as the Cross was secondary to doing God's will. The saving remnant were the spiritually valiant.

Through creative use, the spiritually valiant turned defeat into victory, turned weakness into strength. They responded to the situation rather than merely reacting to it. They overcame evil with good. They lived by a higher law. Their motivation was "for the Master's sake." So the disciples and the Church may live in spite of circumstance, for such circumstance can reveal spiritual strength as well as physical weakness.

This sermon can help the listener to live beyond a feeling of

---

[1] Adapted from "Valiant Behavior," in *The American Pulpit Series*, Book VII (New York and Nashville: Abingdon Press, 1945). Used by permission.

weakness in the face of seemingly insurmountable circumstance. It can help him to find the spiritual resources he needs for life. As H. G. Wells said, "Until a man has found God and been found by God, he begins at no beginning, he works to no end." This sermon reveals that greater power for the valiant life, the power to become the sons of God.

III

Sometimes persons develop inferiority feelings because of handicaps. They are so aware of physical inadequacies, for instance, that they fail to realize their mental and spiritual potential. The following sermon by Walter L. Cook deals with the adjustment to and creative handling of handicaps.

HANDLING YOUR HANDICAPS [2]

Text: *"There was given to me a thorn in the flesh."*—II Cor.12:7

We are all handicapped in some way or another, visibly or invisibly. Some are aware of their own handicaps and the handicaps of others more quickly because they are physical. But some handicaps of education, environment, disposition, or unseen ailment may be just as important a factor in the living of life.

Paul had the ability to use a handicap. He kept it in proper focus and never lost sight of its relative size. A thorn may be small in size but large in its nuisance value. Life may be so conscious of its thorns that it loses sight of all the rest. Paul developed a capacity to keep plodding on in spite of the thorn because he felt that God's grace was sufficient for him.

A piano can be an instrument for discord or for harmonious music. It is not so much the instrument as how it is used that counts. Many persons have to adjust to circumstances but it can be done without self-destruction. A teacher who was forced to give up personal ambi-

[2] Adapted from "Handling Our Handicaps," *The Upper Room Pulpit,* September, 1950. Used by permission.

tions because of family responsibilities was able to pass on her vision to a class that produced several famous educators. A diamond is set on black velvet to display it, but the very fact of overcoming its contrasting background makes it show more brilliantly. So also with those who accomplish in spite of handicap. They learn to work, play, pray, and struggle on to win the crown of life. They are the great heroes.

> *He alone is great*
> *Who by a life heroic*
> *Conquers fate.*[3]

In this sermon the preacher starts with those who may feel sorry for themselves and use their self-pity to evade responsibility and creative living, and he brings them face to face with their larger opportunity, the chance to use their handicap as a basis for an even finer witness. For those who feel inferior because of handicaps, the sermon speaks directly to the special danger of using a handicap as an escape rather than as a background against which one can reach a greater achievement.

[3] Sarah Knowles Bolton, "The Inevitable." Used by permission.

CHAPTER XIII

Preaching to Those Gripped by Injurious Habits

It is inevitable that we will preach to persons who are gripped by a pattern of behavior that injures them. Often they are aware of the injurious effect and want to break the pattern. At other times they do not sense the cause of injury and make diffused expressions of their concern over the effects without seeing the causes. To illustrate, there are two persons with the same injurious habit. One, intelligent and otherwise likable woman, has created an undesirable reputation because she talks too much. She doesn't have anything of particular interest to say, but from the moment she meets people until they leave she pours out an unending flow of verbal trivia. She knows people avoid her and says she wishes she could learn not to talk too much. She is in the grip of an injurious habit, but she does not understand that it is an anxiety, a fear that she may have to suffer from the words of others, which causes her to put up a barrage of words that no one can break through. When she can understand that her fear is no longer warranted and that people would say pleasant things if she would listen, she might move beyond the habit that is crippling her human relations.

The other person, a clergyman, has much the same habit with

much the same sort of reaction from other people. Yet he seems to believe that every word he utters is the essence of profundity. When anyone gets within earshot he starts to pontificate on whatever subject seems to be most pertinent. According to his own words, he is an expert on all matters. Persons who go to him with problems never get a chance to say anything because he is so busy with his own ideas and words. He obviously enjoys listening to what he has to say. Most of what he says would be valuable if properly used, but he injures his personal relations and his ministry by such intemperate use of his own words. Members of his parish avoid him because they find it difficult to break in on him to say they have another appointment. Certainly, his problem would be more difficult to approach because he does not seem to sense it. He would have to be brought to take an over-all look at himself and his human relations before he would begin to sense either the problem or its cause. Both would be essential to a solution.

Such problems present a challenge to the preacher, for he must develop a technique that can approach the minds and hearts of such persons so that their resistance is minimized and their insight is increased. Perhaps it is of primary importance to operate with a full understanding of a new knowledge we have of habits and their workings. There was a time when it was felt that injurious habits were the result of carelessness or willfulness. Now it is more fully understood that habits may be the response to subconscious motivations, fears, or mechanisms of defense that may be operative. The bad habits of the gossip may be a method of defense against a sense of guilt and the fear that others may read the marks of error on the gossip's own soul unless attention can be diverted. The habitually late person may injure himself through a device he has developed to show resentment against those who would try to fit his life into a mold that is unacceptable. In such cases the habit cannot be effectively handled by a direct approach but rather there must be a thorough understanding of the cause.

The human personality is a composite of patterns of behavior. Certain people do things in certain ways. Because we know their patterns of response, we feel we know them. We feel secure with another person when we feel we are able to predict this behavior and depend on these habitual responses. Good habits or dependable responses make what we call a good person. Injurious habits or unacceptable response patterns make what we call an undependable person. Yet we know very well that many injurious habits are not willful or even conscious. We recognize that fact in the case of tics or mannerisms. We are not so likely to realize it with what might be called psychic tics or mannerisms. We do not really come to grips with the problems of many persons until we recognize that some of their injurious behavior falls within this category and must be dealt with, not as a matter of blame, but as a matter of healing revelation.

Then, too, there are the variables of conscience that have to be taken into consideration. There are some things considered injurious in one environment that are accepted as normal in another. Many of our young men who found certain types of behavior acceptable and not socially injurious in the military framework of life have come to realize that the same patterns of behavior are not tolerated and are socially injurious in the civilian community.

The conflict between the mature conscience and the immature, or inherited, conscience also has an influence on what is injurious and what is not. Just the element of anxiety created by such a conflict can be injurious to a person unless he can be helped to resolve that inner battle. A personality does not reach maturity until he is able to operate in decision-making circumstances on the basis of his own moral judgments, not those that have been passed down to him without his examination or real acceptance. During adolescence most persons go through the process of testing the moral standards they have inherited. They seem to question the values and behavior of others and often stand in open rebellion. Such are the symptoms of the emergence of the individual conscience. To a certain extent it is a healthful sign. The completely submissive and subservient youth at that age is a cause for much more concern, for he is apt to put off too long this matter of developing his own conscience. When the process is postponed the conflict is likely to be more detrimental to the personality, and the visible behavior patterns may be more universally rejected. This is the type of person who becomes suspicious, subtly vindictive, emotionally undependable, and excessively demanding in the area of human relations.

The preacher can help to encourage the development of the type of maturity that will minimize injurious behavior by giving insights to parents of adolescents, on the one hand, and to the adolescents themselves, on the other, so that this period of growth can be accepted with as much mutual understanding as possible.

Many habits that are viewed as injurious are the visible signs of an inadequate conscience. Excessive indulgence of the appetites may injure health and home relationships. These can often be related to emotional needs that are unsatisfied normally. A compulsive appetite for sweets is often related to a need for love and emotional support that is diverted. A compulsive thrift may result from a concept of money as a soul-satisfying value rather than as a means toward more useful ends. Similarly, a compulsive spending pattern may be a symptom of an emotional insecurity that is continually trying to buy the love and support of others. Such habits cannot be handled directly with lasting effectiveness.

The solution lies not with the behavior itself but with the needs that prompt the behavior.

The pulpit can be both an instrument in helping people to grow into a more adequate and mature set of values, on the one hand, and in giving them a capacity to bring injurious habits under rational control, on the other. But it places a heavy demand on preaching. The unrestrained condemning of human faults, with no guidance as to how to deal with them, leads to frustration and despair. The stimulation of strong desires for right relations with self and others that does not lead to practical application may be falsely reassuring and lead to even more despair. The pulpit can approach human problems with a recognition of the different origins of behavior. The problems of conscience involved in the parable of the Prodigal Son can illustrate this point. Jesus was able to make clear the difference between the youth who found himself and the youth who stayed home with an unhealthy and immature conscience. So also in the parable of the Good Samaritan, Jesus separates the devices of the immature conscience—as used by the lawyer, the priest and the Levite—from the more mature reactions of the Samaritan, the innkeeper, and the narrator himself. In this way people are helped to participate in a growth experience, an act of self-exploration, and move on to new attitudes and actions.

While being thoroughly aware of the factors involved which complicate the picture of the workings of conscience, the preacher must also help persons to recognize the subtle forces at work to make them compromise the values they have willingly adopted but are likely to neglect. The values of the good life are not established once and for all. They must be continually worked on so that they become clear and useful rather than confused and tarnished.

Early in his ministry Jesus was faced with the problems of the compromise of moral values. Was he to use his spiritual resources to achieve those ends that were related to his physical satisfaction? He moved beyond the satisfactions of appetite to the large standard of God's will. Those who come before us are continually tempted to slip into habits of mind that will injure their spiritual life. Sometimes these attitudes relate to sex indulgence that threatens the security of the home. Sometimes they relate to business practices that threaten integrity. Again they may be very personal in nature but threaten to impair usefulness. In dealing with such things people need to have clearly presented the alternatives of *knowing* and *doing* God's will.

Also there is the temptation to use power for purposes that are not in accord with God's plan. In our power-conscious world there is an ever present temptation to think primarily in terms of power politics, power finance, and power control. Usually the invitations to use such power are given with the promise of more than is possible. Jesus knew well that the promise, "all power shall be given if," was an overstatement of the case. Many of our people are faced with a chance to achieve so-called success in return for demands on life so great that family, church, and community suffer. At these points they need to have the values of life continually clarified.

Then there is the subtle danger of misusing the power of religion. We know of the power of prayer, but we also know of its abuse. We know of the uses of piety that are worthy and those that are unworthy. We know of the temptations that come to use religion as an escape from responsibility rather than a way to it. We know of the temptation to use the spectacular and the superficial rather than the patient and self-sacrificing approach to human need. We know how easy it is to seek short cuts to the Kingdom rather than follow the way of that cause-effect relationship that Jesus adopted even though it led to a cross.

We need also to recognize the power of the temptations which bind men and women to habits that they know are injurious and that call for a clearer concept of the values of life and religion to help them break their slavery.

In dealing with both the compulsive types of behavior and the type that wilts before the pressure of persistent temptation, the pulpit can work constructively at three points. It can preach in a way that will enable people to stand off and look at themselves as they are. Also the sermon can be prepared to help both the troubled and those related to them to understand the areas of conflict in conscience so they can deal with them constructively. And finally, the pulpit can help people to attain and maintain a greater degree of moral maturity by understanding the nature of moral values and the importance of maintaining them. These three types of approach are illustrated by the following sermon résumés.

I

The following sermon might be used to help create the mood for self-examination and understanding of the patterns of behavior that are injurious.

THE POWER TO SEE YOURSELF

Text: *"Search me, O God, and know my heart: try me, and know my thoughts: and see if there be any wicked way in me, and lead me in the way everlasting."*—Ps. 139:23-24

This is the prayer of a man who would examine himself. All of us come upon the realization at one time or another that "the fault is not in our stars, but in ourselves." So first, he calls upon God for the objectivity that God alone can give.

Second, he seeks understanding of his heart, the seat of emotions. The emotions are often elusive, and deep and prayerful study is needed to gain an insight into their function and their effect upon our living.

Third, he seeks to examine his mind and the thoughts that come into it, for the disciplined mind that understands emotions can help to bring them into a proper relationship.

Fourth, he wants to know what is disruptive of life so that he may be led beyond it to secure and eternal values.

Such a procedure is important to every man, for only when he knows himself can he begin to control himself; and only when he can control himself will he be a worthy instrument in God's hands for doing God's will.

II

In order to understand how temptation works, and how one can gain a measure of emotional security and self-control, the following sermon may be useful.

THE BIOGRAPHY OF A TEMPTATION
Text: *The story of Balaam and Balak and the ass that led Balaam to understanding.*—Num. 22

The narrative of this story indicates how temptation can come to work in life: first through flattery; then through financial inducement and the promise of special privilege; and finally through a willingness to compromise—to see only a part of the picture or a part of the truth.

Then the strange behavior of the ass brings Balaam back to his senses and he sees how he came close to being a false prophet.

The story can be easily applied to the situations of life that flatter and offer financial reward, and all for a seemingly reasonable compromise. But compromise is cumulative, and those who would serve God and find life's deeper meaning must see clearly, speak with sober judgment, and accept the consequences.

148

III

Hazen G. Werner speaks to those who are confused or weakened in conscience as well as to those concerned about such persons. Here he not only indicates a sense of direction but gives inspiration to move in that direction.

KEEP THE FAITH THAT KEEPS [1]

Text: *"I have kept the faith. . . . The Lord stood with me, and strengthened me."*—II Tim. 4:7-17

Paul wrote to his young friend Timothy about the importance of keeping his faith vital, for it is the vital faith that sustains life in times of temptation and crisis. In spite of numerous failures among those upon whom he had depended, Paul kept on toward his goal, sustained by faith. Now at the end of life he could say, "I have finished my course, I have kept the faith."

The faith that we keep, keeps us. If we bear the cross it will soon bear us.

What you do makes you what you are. The quality of personality is not built by circumstance and experience alone, though they help, for actually what we are determines what the experience of life will do to us. The more we devote ourselves to good purposes, the easier it becomes for us to respond to that which is worth while.

Whatever gets your attention gets you. Life is an investment. If we invest in fear and worry we receive our returns in increased fear and worry. If we invest in faith, we produce faith and its benefits. If your religion does not mean enough to you, it probably means you have not meant enough to your religion.

Keep the faith that keeps. Live by it. It will sustain you.

In this sermon the preacher deals with practical reality. God does not promise an easy campaign with sure victory in every battle, but he does give strength to face the battle with honor.

---

[1] Adapted from "Keep the Faith that Keeps" in *Real Living Takes Time* (New York and Nashville: Abingdon Press, 1948). Used by permission.

CHAPTER XIV

Preaching to the Aged

The American congregation is getting older all the time. Due to better diet and medical care and the declining death rate, life expectancy is increasing. Paul was an old man at fifty-five because the life expectancy in his day was only twenty-three. Now a man of fifty-five is considered to be in the prime of his life. At the turn of the century the expectancy for life was under fifty years. At mid-century it was getting close to seventy years. Over twelve million people in our population are now sixty-five years of age or older. These persons represent a large portion of those who attend church or listen in to church services. Much consideration has been given in the past to the needs and interests of young people. We must now face the fact that we have as important a responsibility to those over sixty-five as we have to the adolescent members of the parish.

This numerically large segment of our congregation has its problems. Often there is a large measure of financial insecurity, for the pension plans that have been increasingly adopted in recent years do not give adequate coverage to many of these persons. Also, for many of them there is a growing social problem. The architecture of modern America does not provide for them as past generations have done. The large homes of the past made room for parents and aging relatives and gave them a chance to be a useful part of the household. They could do work that was appreciated and at the same time guarantee their physical and emotional security. The limited space of modern homes precludes this type of relationship and other provision must be made. Often this means institutionalization and here again there is a variety of problems that can disturb our elders. This is evidenced by the simple fact that a quarter of the first hospital admissions to mental institutions comes from this group, which represents less than seven per cent of the total population. Many of our older people are disturbed persons and the church has a ministry to them.

Preaching to those who are aged or aging calls for an understanding of their special needs. Socially, there is fear of rejection and exclusion from the life they have known. Physically, there is increased limitation on strength and a variety of those ailments that are a part of the wearing out of the physical organism. The contracting circle of friends is a disturbing fact to many. The fears of the complete reordering of life which living in an institution entails is a disheartening prospect. The spiritual needs of those who must not only come face to face with their waning strength, but must also face the experience of death, are clearly defined and real. The fear of long-drawn-out illness, with the thought of outliving financial resources, is a constant worry to many. The fear of becoming a burden also troubles many older persons. The uncertainty about faith and questions about immortality, as well as feelings of guilt and remorse, may increase with age and create moods of depression. Concern about the unfinished tasks of life may cause consternation. For some the inability to accept retirement is a serious problem. For all, the concern for using the rest of life to full advantage is a present reality. Preaching to older members requires a consciousness of all these factors and a sympathetic response to the feelings and concerns that are bred by such problems.

For some, the older years are a triumphant and satisfying reality. They would resent a pitying attitude toward them. They are finding a fulfillment for life that they have long deserved. They have the inner resources to meet it with joy and usefulness. In preaching to the problems of the aged it is important to keep in mind the privileges, and those who have so well claimed those privileges. Preaching must in some way seek to confirm the faith of those who have found the older years good, and at the same time an effort must be made to reveal such a meaning to those who have not yet found them so.

What then can be the gospel that we preach to the aged? While there must be emphasis on the promises of faith, there must also be a careful avoidance of the trivial reassurance that is patently false. Spiritual values that are essential for all of life are increasingly meaningful to the aged, who have outlived many of the merely material satisfactions of life. The renewing of the spirit can help to bring new interests into life. When Longfellow was asked, late in life, how it was that he was able to keep his youthful interest in all about him, he invited his questioner to look out of the window at an apple tree in full blossom. Then he inquired, "Where are the blossoms?" His questioner looked closely and said, "On the new wood." Longfellow had learned the art of growing new wood, and it was the new wood that brought the new interests. The older years give opportunity for many of the interests and activities that younger years had to postpone. The ability to keep growing new experience makes the days and years blossom with new acquaintance and new activity.

Preaching can continually open up new frontiers of experience that may become inviting to the aged. Emphasis may be placed on the development of a capacity for enjoyment. Too often per-

sons live their lives so busily that they never learn to enjoy things
or people. Retirement gives a chance to learn a new set of attitudes toward life, and it is possible to "teach old dogs new tricks."
All that is needed is adequate incentive. Too often, loss of
memory is not so much a matter of loss of ability as much as
it is loss of interest. If the older years can be filled with new
interests, all of life is vitalized. The older years can open opportunities for human relations, creative employment, and creative
recreation. One pastor, in speaking of the needs of children in
a day nursery, caught the imagination of a man recently retired.
He opened a toy shop in his garage and persons from far and
near bring him broken toys to mend. He has found a new life
centered about children who love him and help keep him young.

Preaching to the older members of the congregation often calls
for slightly different language. So often we try to catch the
words and phrases of youth in order to hold the interest of
youth. It is also important to build into the context of the sermon
those words, phrases, and illustrations that make the older persons feel a sense of "at homeness." The pulpit utterance that is
related to their mental furnishings, their familiar words and concepts, the experiences that have been a part of their life, saves
them from the unpleasant feeling of being excluded. Here as
elsewhere, one of the emphases our Master would stress would
be to avoid that which causes a separation either in feeling or
experience.

Preaching to those in homes for the aged gives specialized
opportunity. Many of us are involved in conducting regular
services in such homes. Here one can almost sense the mood of
the institution as he enters. Sometimes there is a disquieting
sense of quiet resignation. At other times there is a vitality,
a humor, a sense of relatedness that is refreshing. The service
will be related to the mood and the needs that are reflected.

Older people do not want to be treated as such specifically. It becomes another act of separation from the normal stream of life. Rather, they would prefer to be dealt with in friendly, direct terms as people for whom the central truths of the Christian gospel have a sure relevance.

Usually such services should not be over half an hour in length, with old familiar hymns, and a talk that is narrative in nature and direct in appeal. Although humor must be used with care, it is often stimulating to see the response that older persons will make when the humor is well within their range of interest and response. Also, because many have difficulty in hearing, it is important to speak slowly and distinctly and louder than in other circumstances, though the loudness is not so important if the words are clear and slowly spoken. To speak so that one is not heard brings but another experience of frustrating exclusion to the audience.

Leslie Weatherhead, in speaking especially to the aged of his parish, used a sermon on "The Last of Life." Taking as a scriptural theme the words, "The inward man shall be renewed," he spoke of the privileges of growing old to claim the best of life for which the rest was lived. He emphasized that, although the peak of physical accomplishment may have been passed for these members, the quality of the spiritual life and the insight of the mind could continue to increase.

Weatherhead made four specific points. (1) The older years are as normal as any other years and the spiritual invitations as pertinent as ever. The words of Jesus to "follow me" are not limited to any age group. (2) There should be an honest facing of the demands that change entails. We do not fight against inevitable reality. We accept it and grow through it. It is tragic for an older person to try to cling to some of the aspects of youth. It becomes an act of foolishness. Similarly, one does not retire

154

until one has prepared his spirit for the adventure that retirement can bring. (3) Older members should realize the assets of their years. Youth is right about some things, but so also is the insight of the older adult. Mature wisdom is needed at many points in life and the older statesmen have much to contribute. (4) We ought to think a little about death, not to become preoccupied with it, but to become gradually acquainted with the idea. Prepare for it as for any normal experience. "Days are as grass." "With old age will I satisfy thee," but that satisfaction is a prelude to death itself. If a person can develop an understanding of the natural processes involved, such as the relation of autumn and winter, his fears will be quelled, and he can lie down at night with the calm feeling, "It will be a lovely day tomorrow."

Perhaps this approach of Weatherhead and of the three sermon résumés that follow may be helpful and suggestive for use with general congregations having older members, or for use in homes for the aged where the age group is more sharply defined.

I

The authority of the Scriptures is important soul nourishment for the aged, who can read at their own tempo and without regard to hearing loss. The first sermon uses the appeal to scriptural promises to help sustain the spirits of the aged listener, as well as create the perspective of a long life with its rich blessings.

THE WELL-NOURISHED FAITH

Text: *"I have been young, and now am old; yet have I not seen the righteous forsaken, nor his seed begging bread."*
—Ps. 37:25

The word of God is rich with promises that relate to the spirit nourished by faith. It is the experience of life that many of the things we worry about never happen, and those that do happen are not affected in a helpful sense by any amount of worry. Faith can help to relieve life of its unworthy worries.

The writer of the text takes the long look at life that only the person of mature years has the privilege of taking. The more he sees of life, the more is his faith verified. The faith that is good for the young is even better for the aged.

Fulfillment of life is a privilege and not a threat. There is spiritual nourishment to satisfy all of the needs of life, whatever the age. The fruits of long life may well be the deepened and enriched faith that becomes an adequate threshold for the promises of immortality.

The well-nourished soul has an inner adequacy that is fit for long life. Yet the task of continuing to nourish our souls persists. We should not be guilty of neglect at this point, for these are the days in which many of the spiritual promises can be claimed.

The circle of friends and interests decreases with advanced years. But as the circle becomes smaller the individual at the center needs to depend more and more upon his inner resources. This sermon seeks to indicate some of the resources that can be depended upon and interprets their relation to the needs of the advancing years.

II

Often the person who faces retirement dreads what he thinks will be empty years. They are empty only if the mundane activities of the years have crowded out some of the idealism and spiritual interests that youth had known. Now is the opportunity to restore them.

THE SPRINGS OF SPIRITUAL LIFE

Text: *"Arise, go up to Bethel, and dwell there."*—GEN. 35:1

There came a time in the life of Jacob when the limited loyalties of his life proved to be inadequate. Then he had to return to those visions which had sustained him in his youth.

Too often the preoccupations of life obscure the more important spiritual values. There comes a time, with advancing years, when we cannot be satisfied by the trivial and material but must seek to build again the altars that sustain the deepest and best in life.

The routine demands of the middle years of life often tend to dim the visions and to occupy our time and energy with bread and butter tasks. The perspective of the years brings us again to the place where we seek the values that can truly meet our deeper needs.

The older years may become a time for spiritual refreshment, a rebuilding of the altars, and a discarding of the values that are not good enough. Perhaps this is part of the preparation essential to think of life as eternal.

Retirement may bring the time and inclination to arise and return to Bethel, the place where God is.

The story of Jacob is used to bring the mind to focus on the importance of a deliberate and strong effort to use the later years for building spiritual interests that can fit life for its eternal meaning. These are the times when "a closer walk with God" can be realized.

III

Life is a process and the pleasures and privileges of each stage in the process can be revealed to those who would know them. The sermon that follows indicates the mood and direction through which the process can be made a joy rather than a trial.

YOUR DAYS ARE NUMBERED
Text: "As your days, so shall your strength be."
—Deut. 33:25 (R.S.V.)

Often we become so busy with living life as to forget that our days are numbered and that each morning brings opportunities and privileges that will not be repeated. There will be others but never the same ones.

God knows our days are numbered. Do we? If we did how would we invest ourselves during each day?

We have only today. All we can do is take each day as it comes. Sufficient unto each day is the evil thereof, but also equal is the strength that can be given to sustain us through the day.

Compartmentalized living brings a sense of security, for yesterday does not run into today, nor today into tomorrow. We live each day with faith and then are better able to meet tomorrow in the same faith.

Threescore years and ten, even fourscore years, pass quickly. So teach us to number our days that we may apply our hearts to the higher wisdom. The earlier it is done the better, but it is never too late to begin making the most of the day we have.

The aged may not be able to tell too much about tomorrow and dare not dwell too much in the past. To make each day the richest experience possible is a challenge that can help to guarantee life's purpose and interest until its end. This sermon focuses on that possibility.

CHAPTER XV

Preaching to the Immature

Starting with such books as *The Mature Mind,* by Harry Overstreet, and *In Search of Maturity,* by Fritz Künkel, there has been a considerable amount of discussion of the basic meaning of growing up. The popular appeal of such books has been directly related to the feeling of concern that people have for the interpretation of the seemingly irrational elements of their own behavior. That such concern is quite general indicates an opportunity for those who would interpret high religion as being an achievement of the mature mind.

Even before there was a popular interest in such matters by the general reading public, maturity was a matter of consideration for those especially interested in matters of mental health. Maurice Levine, in a psychiatric textbook written before 1942, listed what he considered to be the ten criteria for establishing a descriptive understanding of the mature or normal personality. His concern was with the evidences of an adjustment made by the adult that indicates his reasonable freedom from childish emotional states, dependence, and illusions. But in spite of the fact that he gives a useful and clear definition of the nature and boundaries of mature behavior, he does not indicate how such behavior is to be attained.

Harry Overstreet and his wife have dealt with this problem

in three more recent books. *Understanding Fear in Ourselves and Others, The Great Enterprise,* and *The Mind Alive.* In each instance they have tried to make available to the general reader the understanding of self and social relationships that could make it possible to move beyond immature and restrictive behavior to a calm, discerning, balanced attitude toward life.

Religion at its best has always been concerned with the abundant or the mature life. The parables of Jesus deal again and again with the problems of the truly adult attitude toward self and others. The Rich Young Ruler was invited to see his responsibility in adult terms. The murderous-minded men were invited to look beyond the adulterous woman to the adequacy of their own standards. The disciples were asked to look at the unimpeded process of growth in a young child as a standard for their own continuous growth. In his own life Jesus illustrated the importance of manifold growth in mind, in body, and in favor with God and man. The concept of the abundant life seems to have been less a matter of spiritual grace than a mature and balanced capacity for right relationship with the self, the social matrix, and the Creator.

The preacher has an unusual chance to interpret the nature of the Christian religion as being a concern for this fabric of mature right relationships. He is in a position to make the burden of his pulpit ministry an emphasis upon the acts and attitudes that reveal this capacity for mature relationships. While such an emphasis would not be explicit in every sermon, it would surely be implicit. So important a message demands that he begin the preaching of it with a sharp self-examination. Too often the ministry becomes a retreat for the immature. The preaching that is the product of such immaturity may well be damaging to those who are subject to it. Karl Stolz, in *The Church and Psychotherapy,* has given a chapter to the careful evaluation of the pastor's own emotional life as it relates to his pastoral functions. Every minister would do well to take the kind of spiritual and emotional inventory that Stolz suggests in that chapter.

The preacher, in his relationship to his people, is well aware of the variety and the nature of the problems that concern them. He should be aware of those that are related to immature attitudes in order to deal with them clearly and tactfully in his preaching program. He cannot fail to observe the problems that immaturity projects into the personal relations of his people, their family, and their church activity. He can usually tell rather soon who are the oversensitive, the self-centered, and the touchy individuals in the group. Their immaturity in relation to others is readily apparent. Those who baby themselves and surround their living with a cushion of self-pity project their inner problems into their group activities. Such immaturity can be recognized in the religious thinking of members of the parish.

Those who must at all cost protect the crude structure of absolutist religious ideas and force them upon others are revealing their inability to sense and value the spiritual insights of others. Their only security is to protect themselves from the demands of growth that contact with the ideas of others would involve. So they will commit themselves to believe the unbelievable, to champion the irrational, to defend the improbable— all in order that they will not have to accept responsibility for a painful growth of their own religious ideas. A few such persons seem to be a part of every parish, and their attitude indicates the need for patient understanding of the emotional factors that make them so fearful of spiritual growth.

The pastor, in his preparation for preaching, needs to be aware of the symptoms that immaturity wears. Lack of perspective, limited patience, poor balance between dependence and independence, self-centeredness, and intolerance—all are evidence of impeded emotional and spiritual growth. Quick action in terms of immediate goals, rather than considered action with long-range values in mind, characterizes the impulsive and immature person. Repressed behavior on the basis of a childish conscience, rather than ability to move easily in terms of adult privileges and responsibilities, is a further sign of immature behavior. Inability to love some other person or persons, as well as a fear of making decisions that must be made, indicates emotional immaturity. The inability to relax and enjoy the pleasures of life that one is entitled to enjoy indicates an immature attitude just as much as the laziness that is unwilling to accept reasonable responsibility. All of these types of behavior may indicate to the pastor the presence of the kind of emotional problems that he can help to deal with through his discerning pulpit utterance.

But the pastor needs to know more than the symptoms of emotional immaturity. He must be able also to sense the process of normal growth, since his effort will be to protect growth where it is normal and to stimulate it where it is impeded. As a part of his make-up, every normal adult has many of the emotional satisfactions of earlier periods of growth. The infant is characterized largely by his appetite. A baby will normally consume a fourth of his weight in a day. For an adult to attempt such a feat would be far from normal—it would be destructive. But often the emotional satisfactions of such early days of life can carry over, and the major satisfaction of life may come from ravenous and intemperate eating or drinking. While it is normal and good for an adult to have a good appetite and enjoy his food, it is unfortunate if he lives to eat rather than eats to live.

An early impulse is related to acquisitiveness and the emotional satisfactions that come from the creation and possession of things. While it is good for the adult to have a healthy sense of the

162

importance of things, it is unfortunate if he is so obsessed by the accumulation of things that he has no place for values or the satisfactions of human relations. So also there can be a preoccupation with physical sensation. While every adult is entitled to share the sensations that bring to life a sense of its beauty, comfort, and pleasure, it is unfortunate indeed when the main quest of life is for pleasurable sensations. When such states exist in the physically adult individual it is an indication that the emotional growth is regressed or impeded at a childhood level of satisfaction. Sometimes this requires specialized psychotherapy, but with many persons a new sense of understanding of their emotional life can help to bring them toward more adult satisfactions.

Increasingly, those who work with emotional problems feel that it is not necessary to retrace all of the steps of the emotional life to bring insight. Long and expensive analysis is often ineffective and may be indicated only in the most deep-seated form of disturbance. Being used more widely is the practice of dealing directly with the symptoms and stimulating the adult mind to come to grips with its problem specifically. This brings the whole process much nearer to the sort of thing that can be done through the sermon.

At many points the Scriptures deal with the major emotional manifestations of the immature. The concern for the appetite-dominated life is found in both the Old and New Testaments. The sharp criticism of the thing-conscious view of life is made by the Prophets as well as the New Testament writers. The irresponsible search for sensation is continually brought into comparison with the selfless acceptance of responsibility. There is important scriptural precedent for dealing with the major evidences of emotional immaturity. The tradition of the Christian pulpit has long used a direct approach to these matters. It is now possible, with a finer insight into the personality dynamics related to such emotional states, to make preaching a keener instrument in dealing with the problems of personality created by such immaturity.

When emotional satisfactions are regressed, when the crying approach to life is adopted, when there is fear of change toward more mature standards of life, then the pulpit has the more direct responsibility for helping people to sense what is causing their problem and encouraging them to deal with it wisely. Thus they gain a perspective concerning themselves and the courage to make the changes that the vision of a more abundant life demands. Also, it is well to keep in mind that the process of growth is an eternal challenge. The choices of life keep coming at us and the ability to respond to them with maturity and wisdom is not predicated on any simple formula but rather by a program of continual self-searching and creative relationship with the lives and needs of others.

In the sermons that follow we see how these matters have been approached by preachers who were aware of the problems and tried to deal with them constructively, either by a direct approach or by the oblique approach that could involve the mind and emotions without making the immediate objective explicit.

I

Russell L. Dicks, with his understanding of the emotional forces that work in personality, has developed a sermon about the basic religious affirmations but has brought to bear the psychological insight that calls into question the false standards to which many persons cling. All through this sermon there is the invitation to grow toward more mature values, but the subject of maturity or growth is scarcely touched upon directly.

DRAW NEAR AND BELIEVE [1]

Text: *"My flesh and my heart faileth: but God is the strength of my heart, and my portion for ever. . . . It is good for me to draw near to God."*—Ps. 73:26-28

Early we learn that pleasure is good and what hurts is bad. But we also learn that values are built out of an understanding of opposites. Hunger makes food good. Cold makes warmth good. Loneliness makes friendship good.

Often it is difficult to understand the mysteries of God. How can we explain tragedy? We can only begin to deal with it effectively when we move beyond the area of physical satisfactions. It takes the well developed spirit to be able to respond creatively to the tragedies of life.

When we come to basic reality we find that science and religion agree. The basic facts and the basic feelings somehow are compatible. But the great insights of life are larger than the limited judgments that we pass. We use electricity though we do not understand it and cannot define it. To insist on full understanding before use would rule out most of life. We cannot wait for such complete understanding. We proceed on the basis of the faith that brings essential fact and essential feeling into a close working relationship.

The invitation to draw near and believe is predicated on the evidence of a dependable universe. Our task is not so much to disprove intellectually as it is to use actually. Then we bring to all of life a power that can draw us closer to the realization of our major needs in life. "God is the strength of my heart. . . . Draw near and believe."

In this sermon the warmth of personal understanding is added to the authority of scripture and tradition to bring about a state of mind that is in accord with the best insights of modern psychology. But even here the emphasis is on a faith that moves

[1] Adapted from "Draw Near and Believe," *The Upper Room Pulpit*, January, 1950. Used by permission.

beyond what can be established by scientific proof. It calls for both mature living and mature religious insight.

II

Using quite a different approach, Halford E. Luccock deals with the problem of perspective and growth. He urges upon his hearers that they develop the adult capacity to distinguish between the real and the imaginary.

STREET LIGHTS OR STARS [2]

Too often in life we cruise with low visibility. This is dangerous. We need to take our bearings on the stars as well as the street lights. We need to relate ourselves to the "kindly light" that was so real to Cardinal Newman.

Mont Blanc is seldom seen among the clouds, but it is there nonetheless. So also the moral laws that govern the universe. They cannot be ignored. For when street lights burn out the stars burn on.

When Louis Blériot flew the English Channel in 1904 an editorial comment said: "This spells the end of nationalism. You cannot have little national units in a world where you have machines that wipe out national boundaries." That hope burned out because men focused on street lights rather than stars.

When T. E. Lawrence tried to explain hot water faucets to the Arabs he found it difficult because they not only had difficulty conceiving of running water but also doubted the possibility of that which could heat it. Their small perspective called into question what others took for granted.

The person of limited judgment is always calling into question what others take for granted. Consequently, he limits his capacity for insight, power, and happiness. Some things must be a part of creative experience rather than destructive analysis based on small

[2] Adapted from "Street Lights or Stars," *The Upper Room Pulpit*, May, 1951. Used by permission.

premises. When two psychologists married it was difficult for them to get along because they gave too much time to analyzing each other and too little time to loving each other. Their relationship was a perpetual post-mortem instead of an act of devotion. Marriage can be built only on an act of faith that accepts and understands.

The small basis of judgment always stands in the way of the larger basis for action. We need to grow in our understanding until the basic premise of life is: "My meat is to do the will of him that sent me." Then the rest of life will have its more adequate explanation.

This sermon pricks the balloon of self-satisfied judgments, makes people smile at their own foolishness, and invites them to grow in the over-all judgments with which they face life.

III

In the following sermon the preacher uses a series of biographical sketches to illustrate the mature bases for human values.

LIFE'S GREAT INVITATION
Text: LUKE 18:18-30

The first scene is in 1893 in a London law office, and a young man is facing the choice between a lucrative law practice or the trip to South Africa to take the case of some abused fellow countrymen. Gandhi goes to South Africa and starts his way toward great spiritual leadership of his people. His choice is between self and others.

The second scene is at Old Bailey in London in 1670. Here is a young man who is scheduled for the admiralty but is brought to trial because he opposes violence on religious grounds. Not only is a dramatic court scene unfolded, but basic legal precedents are set for human freedom, and William Penn starts on his career as a religious reformer. He chooses principle above privilege.

The third scene is three hundred years before Columbus sailed for America. A rich young man becomes dissatisfied with the tawdry life he has lived. He struggles deep within himself to come to terms with life and decides to devote himself from that time on to bringing love to life in all ways possible. St. Francis not only started a reform movement within the Church, but he also established a basic principle by which all men since that time have measured the comparative value between material things and spiritual values.

The fourth scene is toward the end of the third decade of the Christian Era. A young carpenter faces a rich young man who wants to know the real meaning of life. The carpenter indicates the importance of mastering life rather than being mastered by it. He illustrates in his own living that such mastery over life is achieved only by becoming subject to the Creator of all life. So he is able to respond to the best in himself and in those about him. Jesus chose the more abundant life, that of being mastered by God so that he could master himself.

In this type of sermon the dramatic narrative carries the message. The hearer becomes emotionally involved in each episode and senses the contrast of values between his own life and the life of the person who has made the more mature choice. The stimulus to the growth experience is related to mind as well as emotions.

CHAPTER XVI

Preaching on Family Problems

Everyone in our day who is at all informed is aware of the growing tensions in family life that reflect themselves in emotional disorders and in the breakdown of the home through separation, divorce, or annulment. Those who are as closely related to human problems as the pastor are especially aware of the magnitude of the problem that society faces at this point. Some have estimated that a quarter of all marriages will break up and that another quarter are in serious difficulty, so much so that they are not bringing the members of the home the satisfactions that are essential to a normal and happy existence. This would mean that about half of our families are in serious difficulty.

There is reason to believe that the percentage of breakdown among church-related families is below the national average. One survey indicated that when husband and wife went together to the same church and took their religious life seriously there was a 600 per cent better chance for them to escape the marriage courts than for their nonchurchgoing neighbors. This indicates only the overt difficulty that has reached the legal stage. Such a survey does not indicate the tension that may exist among those who are trying to use all of their moral power to maintain their marriage. But it does give us good reason to believe that the church is able to minister effectively at this point.

The church must have a positive message to bring to the home in our day. It must be a message aware of the increasingly important function of the home as a spiritual institution. It must be a constructive message, for there is already too much condemnation with too little understanding of the personality conflicts which plague the homes of our people. One need only look at the architecture of our modern homes to sense how great has been the transformation of its function. In the multiple unit housing developments the out-of-door spaces are figured on the basis of five hundred persons to the acre. Actually, there is more room for living in a cemetery than is provided in those multiple unit housing projects being built in our day. It takes little imagination to know what this means for those who live together in cramped and overlapping quarters.

Years ago houses were made for group living and space was provided within for many activities. Now the house is small and the garage is large. Not only does this indicate that much activity is provided outside the home, but symbolically the garage may indicate a ready means of escape from a home that fails to meet the basic needs of the persons who dwell therein.

A few generations ago the home was the center of education, social life, religious interest, recreational activity, and often in rural areas, the center of economic life. All of these factors gave to the home a significance as an institution and tended to bind it together. Now nearly all of these activities are centered outside the home and the function of the home as a significant institution suffers in consequence. Not only are people drawn away from the home for most of life's activity, but also the function of the home at many levels is called into question by a conflict of authorities.

It is at just this point that the importance of the spiritual life of the home can be emphasized. The spiritual life of the home carries its own authority. The quality of spirit that pervades the home determines the effectiveness of relationship in every other area. The home is the institution that makes love the law of its life. Here human beings find the highest fulfillment for life. Here their souls are made secure against the conflicts and tensions that may be incident to the rest of life. When love rules the home its members go out in strength and work with understanding and good will, and return in confidence to that which can restore their souls. When love fails at home its members go out in despair, work with a sense of bitterness and frustration, and return for more rejection and defeat.

Though many of the functions of the home have been delegated to other institutions of the community, its central purpose has been more clearly defined by that very process. Now as never before we are able to see the spiritual purpose of the home clearly defined. Now we can begin to see more clearly the importance of the church's relationship to the home at the point where it prepares for, encourages, develops, and sustains the spiritual purpose of the home.

This indicates a responsibility for the pulpit at several points. It is important for those preparing for marriage to understand that anything that is divisive at the spiritual level is an immediate and major threat to the basic function of the home in modern life. More and more of our young people are facing the prospect of marriages where different religious faith and practice are involved. Often they feel that this matter is relatively insignificant and that it can be ignored with impunity. One need only face the quiet tragedy and despair that is a part of so many mixed marriages to see that breakdown of the home as a spiritual unit threatens at the very points where the home has its most significant function in modern life. It is of great importance that the pulpit deal informatively and objectively with the issues likely to affect the marriages of those who become so involved.

The pulpit can also deal constructively with the child-parent relationships that are actively disturbing many homes. The changes in our social life are so rapid that there is little continuity of patterns of behavior from one generation to the next. We are not like primitive societies, whose patterns and rituals for emerging from childhood into adulthood are clearly defined. We have few clearly defined folkways, and the variations from family to family and community to community quite naturally generate tensions and misunderstandings. It is at this point that parents often lose sight of long-range goals of personality growth and revert to attitudes that are more nearly comparable to those they question in their children. The pulpit can serve a useful purpose in dealing with the dynamics of personality growth, especially at the point of the dependence-independence conflict. Parents can be reassured by understanding the more universal nature of some of their problems, and new understanding of the forces at work can help them to proceed within their own homes with more patience, more assurance, and fewer tension-creating attitudes.

There are three or four Sundays during the course of the year when it seems fitting and proper to give a special emphasis to the needs of the family. Instead of the saccharin utterances often indulged in on Mother's Day, there may be a careful study of the mother's role in the spiritual responsibilities of the home. Children's Day gives an opportunity for an interpretation of the dynamics of personality growth, especially as it relates to the growth of religious attitudes. Thanksgiving also is a time when one may deal with the home as the institution that is too easily taken for granted and whose contribution to life we should more adequately recognize. A Student Recognition Day, when college youth participate in the service, may give an opportunity to bridge the gap between the religious feelings of one generation and the next. Christian Family Week gives an opportunity to emphasize more vigorously, from a variety of angles, the values of the spiritual life as they relate to the modern home and its varied problems.

Modern psychology has indicated that the major requirement for health of mind and emotions is a secure love relationship. At this point it supports the spiritual function of the home as the institution that is bound together in mutual respect, understanding, and love because it *is* bound together in mutual respect, understanding, and love for God.

Love is not an accident. Some of the physical attractions that are mistaken for love are apt to be accidental. But the love that sustains life is an achievement of mature minds and feelings that have learned how to relate themselves to the needs and interests of others. This is for most people a learned capacity, and one at which we must work diligently all the days of our lives. The church, and the pulpit as an instrument of the church, have a responsibility to continually teach, interpret, and inspire those feelings and attitudes that can make the growth of love possible.

This calls for an emphasis on self-investment in spiritual values. We cannot buy a quart of good will, a pound of love, or a yard of patience. We can only create such values from within ourselves by genuine effort. These are the values that build love and help to make homes spiritually satisfying. Here is a special mission to the home that the church is peculiarly well suited to perform. The church can help people to know and understand the feelings of others. It can encourage honest evaluation. It can interpret the growth process so that there is not only a willingness to accept growth, but an intelligent cooperation with that process. Also, it can help people to gain the resources that

173

make it possible for them to meet more adequately the inevitable periods of pressure and stress that come in all human relations.

Every time the sacrament of baptism is performed before the congregation it presents an occasion when the pastor can briefly and simply call to mind the obligations of parenthood. Every time a marriage ceremony is performed in the church an occasion exists to remind all present of the sacredness of the vows assumed. Every Sunday the pulpit, with its privileged utterance, has an opportunity directly or indirectly to call to mind those values and attitudes that can best sustain the Christian home and guarantee the rewards that should be a part of Christian home life.

In meeting this challenge, pastors will use differing approaches and varied emphases. The following suggested sermons indicate how some have approached the privilege of preaching to family needs.

I

With a simple and direct approach Hazen G. Werner focuses attention on the home and its emotional health. Not only does he ask for an examination of the symptoms that may reflect ill health in the home situation, he also diagnoses the problem and then moves on for a prognosis and a program of treatment.

EVERYTHING ALL RIGHT AT HOME? [1]

Text: *"They that wait upon the Lord shall renew their strength."*—Isa. 40:31

A simple greeting may become a soul-searching question. In the home we learn our first lessons about life. In it we are more nearly our natural selves than anywhere else. Sometimes we abuse the

[1] Adapted from "Everything All Right at Home?" in *Real Living Takes Time* (New York and Nashville: Abingdon Press, 1948). Used by permission.

privileges afforded by the home. How much do we take for granted in our homes?

The home needs God's grace. Marriage calls for a renewal of strength, a ruggedness that is set for the long journey, an ability to "walk and not faint." Many homes are low in stamina and are fainting because they do not use the spiritual resources that can bring a renewal of the strength of love.

Also the home needs solidarity, a sense of togetherness. Life becomes complete within the love of a home, and this love is not a matter of space or time. It is rather the quality of existence able to sustain persons even though separated by many miles and many months. A new dimension is added to life by true love and its loyalty.

The home needs family religion, not so much as a formality but as a practical, everyday sense of responsiveness to each other because all are able to respond to God. Where the spiritual roots of life are faithfully nourished it is reasonable to expect its fruits.

The listener who has known there was something wrong at home but did not want to admit it, can be helped by this sermon to face the situation and do something about it. This sermon is not just a jolt; it is an indication of the resources that are available to put home life back on a sound foundation.

II

David A. MacLennan speaks directly to parents as those who stand in a place of strategic importance at many points in the development of young life.

PARENTS AS PARTNERS [2]

Text: *"Wherefore they are no more twain, but one."*—MATT. 19:6

Parental oneness does not mean a contract or a physical fact as

[2] "Adapted from "Parents as Partners" in *No Coward Soul* (New York: Oxford University Press, 1949). Used by permission.

much as it means an achievement of comradeship. There is need for a premarital understanding of this mutuality. This can come about through an honest interchange of ideas. Mutuality is not the product of abject submission but, rather, a healthy development of love through mutual respect and the fulfillment together of common purposes.

Parental partnership focuses on bringing up children, and neither partner can escape a full share of this responsibility. Children are a source of hope only if parents fulfill their responsibility to give a framework of love and understanding to life.

Parents need to learn a special skill. Not found in textbooks, this skill grows from a willingness to subordinate selfish interests to the need of all the family. This partnership is nourished by a dependence upon a third member of the firm, who continually gives a higher focus to the interests of life. Homes that are Christian are homes that can build character into life, for the yardstick is not man made but is far more demanding. In a society that is exerting many pressures upon life the Christian home is a major contributor to that adequacy for life that we like to call Christian character.

For those who may have taken their parental tasks lightly, doing what they thought came naturally, there will be the awakening of a new sense of responsibility and a deepened awareness of the importance of all that they do in life. The resources of the Christian faith are specially adapted to those who would understand children and effectively guide their emerging personalities.

III

Each June, the month of many marriages, gives an opportunity for a re-examining of the sacred vows that establish the married relationship, and the elements of carelessness and decay that tend to destroy them.

THE LIFE THAT FAILED

Text: *"What . . . God hath joined together."*—MARK 10:9

Man can never put asunder what God hath joined. But too often man tries to put together those who have no understanding of the union that is in God.

There is the type of union that ignores God. The marriage of convenience, or low purpose, brings forth the bitter fruit of emptiness and frustration.

There is the type of union that defies God. Spiritual disunity at the very core of life shows the inevitable consequences of such defiance. Mixed marriages often come into this category.

Then there is the type of union that forgets God. Concerned by the success of life and its many activities, these couples crowd out God and the church. Then comes the corrosion of life and the inevitable awakening when something valuable and irreplaceable is gone.

But in the type of union that God forms, a priority is given to spiritual things. The growing spiritual basis for life helps to overcome differences, difficulties, and even serious incompatibilities. It guides the way toward the achievement of maturity. It nurtures the young life with a consciousness of its sacred destiny. It prepares the companionship that ripens in advanced years. Truly, such couples *do* live happily ever after.

Marriages may struggle along for years before the spiritual achievement we speak of as union in God becomes a reality. Many couples who are aware of difficulty may need but an invitation to examine their relationship to understand what is lacking and then supply it. The church and the pulpit have a continuing ministry to those whom it would unite most truly.

CHAPTER XVII

And in Conclusion

This excursion into the sacred precincts of preaching has tried to point out some of the resources that are available to the preacher in his approach to people as a result of recent personality studies. New and important tools are available for his use. But it is also important to look briefly at the preacher as the artisan who uses the tools. Throughout, the involvement of the personality of the preacher with the message that he delivers has been recognized. However, it may be helpful in summary to be more explicit at this point.

A number of questions come immediately to mind in considering the relation of the preacher to his message. What is the basic psychological motivation? Why does he preach? What are the satisfactions he gets from preaching? Can he be honest with himself in analyzing these satisfactions, or has he glossed them over with such a thick layer of self-righteousness that he can no longer see himself as he is? If he does not know himself and his motivation, is it probable that he will have a clear idea of what he is doing to other people? An uncertain motivation in the pulpit could be as dangerous as an uncertain hand on the rudder of a boat.

Unfortunate extremes of behavior sometimes occur on the part of preachers. Some seem to get an inordinate satisfaction from scathing denunciation of their hearers. Others fear to speak clearly on any subject lest they become a source of offense. Some give a major emphasis to abstractions because, for them, life itself tends to be abstract, while others concern themselves with specific problems week after week. In any case, the preacher is apt to be reflecting, consciously or unconsciously, the type of concern that is central in his own personality.

The truths of the Christian faith are inevitably affected by the personality that acts as the transmitter. The ministry has more than its share of occupational hazards, and many of them are at the level of the psychological factors that affect the attitude toward self and toward those with whom the minister tries to communicate. These are both affected by the reality and sustaining quality of the relationship that the minister has with God as the source of whatever maturity, empathy, and social awareness he may possess.

The personality structure of a man is well etablished by the time he is in his early twenties. It is for that reason that, increasingly, the authorities of the church are requiring some form of examination that can serve as a personality inventory. Areas of weakness that may make a man a poor risk in the parish ministry need to be known, for the good of the man involved as well as for the good of the ministry in general. Many of the emotional problems that could be troublesome can be corrected at the outset of a professional career. The result would be increased efficiency as well as relief from the unhappiness that often results when a personality must fight against those disturbing psychological "thorns in the flesh."

The occupational hazards that confront a preacher are bound up with his own sensitivity to a source of spiritual power and his capacity for communicating it to others. He may be disturbed by a desire to keep his ministry untouched by commercialization

179

and at the same time meet the financial needs of himself and his family. He may be concerned about his need for warm social contacts, while the nature of his position tends to isolate him. He may be bothered by the fact that much of his work is tentative and indefinite so that specific results are seldom observed. He may be aware of the subtle and corrosive effects of competition with other members of the profession. He may be aware of the lowering of his standards of action in order to gain recognition and immediate emotional satisfaction. He may be conscious of a growing tendency to sit in meditation which is actually laziness and indecision. He may excuse himself from unpleasant duties on the ground that he is too busy with other things and then feel guilty about his indolence. He may lose sight of his goal in his effort to satisfy a number of claims upon him by organizations and people. He may find himself saying what people want to hear because he enjoys the expressions of satisfaction that follow. He may even find himself going out of his way to encourage special consideration for himself as if he were to be served rather than serve. He may even find that in order to preserve a professional front he is involved in building a dual personality, with one set of attitudes for his private life and another set when the parish is involved. All such occupational hazards have an effect on the personality of the preacher and definitely influence his capacity to feel and transmit the spiritual resources that are his concern.

It is a wise procedure for a preacher to set aside certain times each year when he examines himself and his attitudes quite candidly. Thus he may not only guard against the occupational hazards that surround him, but also he may be better able to sense the areas where his own concerns may be conditioning his preaching emphasis. An honest facing of his motivation may be disturbing, but it may also make it possible for him to reclaim and redirect his effort so that the unfortunate may be sublimated and the finer sensitivities redirected and supported. Some object that too careful an examination of the roots of any special gifts they possess may destroy the gift. They indicate that Paul might have lost his great power if he had analyzed too carefully his sense of guilt. Such a suggestion assumes that Paul did not examine his motives rather carefully during the two years he spent in the wilderness and also that his effectiveness might have been dependent on some unresolved neurotic trait. This hardly seems warranted. But even if it were, the sum-total advantages of a carefully considered approach to the ministry would far outweigh any questionable advantages that might accrue from some accidental benefits of disturbed behavior.

One of the unfortunate facts about the professional ministry is that the preacher is so busy serving others that his own emotional and spiritual needs may be neglected. He is so busy helping others to worship that the real experience of worship may not come to him. His reading may be so specifically a search for sermon material that he does not find nourishment for his own soul. He may be so busy on a seven-day-a-week schedule that he fails to take time for rest and recreation. He may be so pressed by financial problems that his spiritual ministry is surrounded by materialistic concerns. He may be so busy developing the inner resources for meeting problems in the lives of other people that he neglects the inner resources he needs to face the problems of his own life.

When such circumstances exist it is important for the preacher to be aware of their implications for his preaching ministry. There should be some responsible, well-qualified, and trusted counselor with whom he could discuss his concerns. There might well be a close and trusted fellowship where preachers could mingle their thoughts and feelings, free from competitive concern and fear of reprisal. Too often the pastoral supervisor is also an administrative authority, and the contradictory functions make ineffective the free access that would be desirable. A cardiologist remarked recently that his practice was made up largely of the clergy and his own fellow physicians. The reason he gave for this was that both professions share so much of other people's problems and anxieties that strength goes out of them; yet they are so busy that they do not find adequate time for restoration, diversion, and relaxation. The physical organism shows the results of the psychic strain. Jesus was wise in that he often took time to go apart a while in a quiet place. Then things came back into perspective: he saw himself as he was, and other people as they were, and God without confusion.

When a minister is able to properly tend his own spiritual life, he can enter the pulpit without fear and misgivings. When he is able to move among his people without false values concerning his own status, or unreasonable judgments concerning theirs, he will be able to communicate from the pulpit with a sense of directness and sensitivity that will generate true responsiveness. Then he will not be uncertain of his motivation or fearful of those quite human impulses that from time to time pass through his mind. He will have the resources to handle them and his central devotion to a clearly defined purpose will keep him well beyond the temptations that might so easily beset him.

It should be pointed out that there are readily available many resources which will help the preacher gain further insight into the nature of personality. Not only is this important for self-understanding, but it helps to give the kind of broad understanding of other people and their problems that can enrich and deepen the quality of preaching. Also there is a sort of moral obligation to keep informed at the point of his professional concern, which is ministering to the needs of people. Two important areas suggest themselves at once. One is the rapidly developing area of counseling, and the other is the work being done in group dynamics.

Much has been written in the field of counseling that is adequate and useful. Because this material helps to give insights into the personalities of people, it is helpful to the preacher. He needs to know problems of people as they are examined by other professional disciplines. However, he needs to beware of too great an emphasis on studies of the abnormal personality, for it might become difficult to see clearly the less complicated needs of those healthy souls who want to be kept healthy.

Clinical and lecture courses are available in some parts of the country and are more useful in most instances than private study. But for an introductory study in the field the following books would be helpful:

Allan, Denison M. *The Realm of Personality*. New York and Nashville: Abingdon Press, 1947.

Dicks, Russell L. *Pastoral Work and Pastoral Counseling*. New York: The Macmillan Co., 1949.

Doniger, Simon, ed. *Religion and Human Behavior*. New York: Association Press, 1954.

Hiltner, Seward. *Pastoral Counseling*. New York and Nashville: Abingdon Press, 1949.

Outler, Albert C. *Psychotherapy and the Christian Message*. New York: Harper & Bros., 1954.

Roberts, David E. *Psychotherapy and a Christian View of Man*. New York: Charles Scribner's Sons, 1950.

Wise, Carroll A. *Pastoral Counseling*. New York: Harper & Bros., 1951.

For a more intensive study of the theory and practice of dynamic psychology the following books would prove to be useful:

Alexander, Franz, *et al. Dynamic Psychiatry.* Chicago: University of Chicago Press, 1952.

Dollard, John and Miller, N. E. *Personality and Psychotherapy.* New York: McGraw-Hill Book Co., Inc., 1950.

Fenichel, Otto. *The Psychoanalytic Theory of Neurosis.* New York: W. W. Norton & Company, Inc., 1945.

Horney, Karen. *Our Inner Conflicts.* New York: W. W. Norton & Company, Inc., 1945.

Levine, Maurice. *Psychotherapy in Medical Practice.* New York: The Macmillan Co., 1942.

Lowrey, L. G. *Psychiatry for Social Workers.* New York: Columbia University Press, 1950.

Menninger, Karl A. *The Human Mind.* New York: Alfred A. Knopf, Inc., 1945.

Reik, Theodor. *Listening with the Third Ear.* New York: Farrar, Straus & Co., Inc., 1949.

Sullivan, Harry Stack. *The Interpersonal Theory of Psychiatry.* New York: W. W. Norton & Company, Inc., 1953.

Thompson, Clara and Mullahy, Patrick. *Psychoanalysis: Evolution and Development.* New York: Hermitage House, Inc., 1950.

Weiss, Edoardo. *Principles of Psychodynamics.* New York: Grune & Stratton, Inc., 1950.

Books that may have a special interest to the preacher because of their historical information and interpretive insight are:

Boisen, Anton T. *The Exploration of the Inner World.* New York: Harper & Bros., 1936.

Fromm, Erich. *Psychoanalysis and Religion.* New Haven: Yale University Press, 1950.

Holman, Charles Thomas. *The Religion of a Healthy Mind.* New York: Round Table Press, 1939.

Kemp, Charles F. *Physicians of the Soul.* New York: The Macmillan Co., 1950.

Lee, Roy S. *Freud and Christianity.* New York: A. A. Wyn, Inc., 1949.

MacLennan, David Alexander. *Pastoral Preaching.* Philadelphia: Westminster Press, 1955.

McNeill, John T. *A History of the Cure of Souls.* New York: Harper & Bros., 1951.

Weatherhead, Leslie D. *Psychology, Religion and Healing* (Rev.). New York and Nashville: Abingdon Press, 1952.

An area of special interest for preachers is the developing research in group dynamics and group therapy. Here many of the principles that have been operative in the preaching relationship are being examined and evaluated with experimental procedures. The findings may encourage the preacher to take a more appreciative look at the function of the healing word spoken to groups, but it may also make him more cautious as he sets himself to the task. Some of the more useful books in this field are:

Cartwright, Dorwin and Zander, A. F. *Group Dynamics, Research and Theory.* Evanston, Ill.: Row, Peterson & Co., 1953.

Hinckley, Robert George and Hermann, L. M. *Group Treatment in Psychotherapy.* Minneapolis: University of Minnesota Press, 1951.

Klapman, Jacob W. *Group Psychotherapy; Theory and Practice.* New York: Grune & Stratton, Inc., 1946.

Konopka, Gisela. *Group Work in the Institution.* New York: Whiteside, Inc., 1954.

Lindzey, Gardner. *Handbook of Social Psychology,* Vol. II. Cambridge: Addison-Wesley Publishing Company, Inc., 1954.

Powdermaker, Florence and Frank, J. D. *Group Psychotherapy.* Cambridge: Harvard University Press, 1953.

Slavson, Samuel Richard. *Creative Group Education.* New York: Association Press, 1937.

Source material that may be useful in dealing with special

problems is available in quantity. The following suggestions might well become the nucleus for a resource library dealing with specific human needs:

ALCOHOLISM

Alcohol, Science and Society. New Haven: Yale School of Alcohol Studies, 1945.

Mann, Marty. *Primer on Alcoholism.* New York: Rinehart & Company, Inc., 1950.

ANXIETY

Hoch, Paul Henry and Zubin, Joseph, eds. *Anxiety.* New York: Grune & Stratton, Inc., 1950.

May, Rollo. *Meaning of Anxiety.* New York: The Ronald Press Company, 1950.

Pike, James A. *Beyond Anxiety.* New York: Charles Scribner's Sons, 1953.

DEPRESSION

Durkheim, Emile. *Suicide, A Study in Sociology.* Translated by John A. Spaulding and George Simpson; edited with an introduction by George Simpson. Glencoe, Ill.: The Free Press, 1951.

Hoch, Paul H. and Zubin, Joseph, eds. *Depression.* New York: Grune & Stratton, Inc., 1954.

Menninger, Karl A. *Man Against Himself.* New York: Harcourt, Brace & Co., 1938.

FAMILY

Erikson, Erik H. *Childhood and Society.* New York: W. W. Norton & Company Inc., 1950.

Fleming, Charlotte Mary. *Adolescence, Its Social Psychology.* New York: International Universities Press, Inc., 1949.

Neill, Alexander Sutherland. *The Problem Family.* New York: Hermitage House, Inc., 1949.

Pollak, Otto, *et al. Social Science and Psychotherapy for Children.* New York: Russell Sage Foundation, 1952.

Symonds, Percival M. *Dynamics of Parent-Child Relationships*. New York: Teachers College, 1949.

Also, studies of the Yale Department of Child Development and of Jean Piaget give useful background for understanding many of the concerns that develop in family life.

Love and Marriage

Bergler, Edmund. *Conflict in Marriage*. New York: Harper & Bros., 1949.

Donahue, Wilma T. and Tibbitts, Clark, eds. *Planning the Older Years*. Ann Arbor: University of Michigan Press, 1950.

Duvall, Evelyn M. *Inlaws: Pro and Con*. New York: Association Press, 1954.

Mead, Margaret. *Male and Female*. New York: William Morrow & Co., 1949.

Menninger, Karl A. *Love Against Hate*. New York: Harcourt, Brace & Co., 1942.

Mudd, Emily. *The Practice of Marriage Counseling*. New York: Association Press, 1951.

In building his basic library on human needs the preacher will want to move slowly and with selectivity. A great amount of material is being printed in this and related fields and not all of it would serve his purpose. Increasingly, the religious publishing houses are handling books with adequate technical background and an orientation in religion that makes them more useful to the pastor.

Also the pastor will want to be more perceptive as to the results of his preaching. It might be well to plan specific sermons to serve specific needs and then try to develop some method for evaluating results. What is the congregational reaction during the actual preaching? How do the comments of the congregation after the service relate to the content of the sermon? Are there requests for copies of the sermon for further study? During the days that follow the preaching of it are there significant counseling relations established? While there are no precise methods for gauging the response to a sermon, a more perceptive use of the methods available might give a clearer picture of just what is going on during the person-to-person relationship that we call preaching.

The preceding pages have made no effort to be exhaustive, definitive, or conclusive. Most preachers, out of their own minds and hearts, will develop their own method of approach and their own modifications of any suggested technique. That is to be expected and desired with any method of communication as personal as that of pulpit utterance. If, however, these pages have served to awaken a new interest in what goes on in preaching, and what may be done to heal the souls of those who come seeking a more abundant life, their purpose will have been served.

INDEX

189

INDEX

191